New & Selected Poems

of

David Waltner-Toews

LYRIK POETRY SERIES 3

Series Editor: Nathan Dueck

New & Selected Poems

of

David Waltner-Toews

Edited and with an introduction
by Nathan Dueck

CMU PRESS
WINNIPEG, MANITOBA
2025

CMU PRESS

CMU Press
Canadian Mennonite University
500 Shaftesbury Blvd.
Winnipeg MB R3P2N2
www.cmupress.ca

CMU Press is learning and striving to create an inclusive and welcoming space for people of many identities and communities. We work on land which is the ancestral home of the Anishinaabe, Cree, Dakota, and Métis peoples. We are grateful for their stewardship of this place.

The publication of this book has received financial support from the Gerhard Lohrenz Publication Fund, administered by Canadian Mennonite University.

Series Editor: Nathan Dueck
Copy editor: Sue Sorensen
Cover and interior design: Jonathan Dyck
Editorial assistance: Javier Jiménez, Chelsea Norton

Printed in Canada by Friesens Corporation, Altona, Manitoba
ISBN: 978-1-987986-17-4

Library and Archives Canada Cataloguing in Publication

Title: New & selected poems of David Waltner-Toews / edited and with an introduction by Nathan Dueck.
Other titles: New and selected poems of David Waltner-Toews
Names: Waltner-Toews, David, 1948- author. | Dueck, Nathan, 1979- editor, writer of introduction
Description: Series statement: Lyrik poetry series ; 3 | Includes bibliographical references and index.
Identifiers: Canadiana 20250141698 | ISBN 9781987986174 (softcover)
Subjects: LCGFT: Poetry.
Classification: LCC PS8595.A61 N49 2025 | DDC C811/.54—dc23

CONTENTS

Introduction

Nathan Dueck

A few years ago, I was struggling to cope with the increasingly dire ravages of climate change, so I turned to Twitter. After venting spleen by asking why anyone would bother to plant a tree in their backyard amid civilization collapse, I received this reply from @DoftWT: "Shouldn't confuse 21st C human civilization with the world. The tree will be there for a future renewal. If the tree dies, the fungi and bacteria will need its nourishment. They will thank you." For possibly the first time in the misbegotten history of social media, someone used their 280 characters to share some wisdom. (As far as I'm concerned, David Waltner-Toews earned his membership in the Order of Canada for that message alone.)

In the canon of Mennonite letters, there's no one like David Waltner-Toews. That could be because there's no *one* David Waltner-Toews. There's Dr. Waltner-Toews, the veterinarian. There's Prof. Waltner-Toews, the epidemiologist. Then there's David, the author of poems, short stories, and monographs. My focus here is on his identity as a poet, although the singular "poet" isn't entirely accurate. In his poetry, Waltner-Toews is a one-man *dramatis personae*. He writes ballads, odes, and dramatic monologues. He composes conversational, occasional, and formal poetry. His subjects span flora, fauna, friends and family, and, ultimately, the concept of community itself. These poems sometimes lecture and ofttimes tease, but they always strike me as sincere—even when being ironic.

COMMUNITY

I could not agree more with Casey Plett's assertion in her recent book *On Community*: "Community. Just the word itself is so damn amorphous . . . Somewhere along the line, such amorphousness has even caused the word *community* to attain semantic satiation for me—the phenomenon in which a word is repeated so often it loses its meaning; it ceases to sound like a word" (14). Although "community" is essential to my thoughts about Waltner-Toews, I cannot claim to know what the word means any more than Plett does. It is not an empty signifier, but at times it seems emptied of any denotative meaning, something like a placeholder. And as far as Mennonites are concerned, we hold that place close to the heart.

Before I have my say about our shared Mennonite community, it seems fair to give Waltner-Toews a chance to speak for himself. In 2006, he contributed an essay to *The New Quarterly* in response to the topic "Falling in Love with Poetry." "It was lust at first glance," he reveals, "a deep, sinful desire for poetry" that developed at the ripe age of ten. But, given that his church would likely condemn such an interest, "it had to be a secret passion" ("What's Love"). Waltner-Toews proceeds to explain how that personal preoccupation informed his professional occupation. Throughout all his work, he concentrates on implications of community, taking into consideration the concept's application to both his cultural heritage and humanity writ large. Working initially as a veterinarian and then an epidemiologist, he has devoted himself to researching possibilities for ecosystem health through community-based solutions. From scholarship about global epidemics to poetry about the domestic sphere, Waltner-Toews demonstrates that, like it or not, we're in this thing together—and the pronoun "we" here includes all living organisms, be they nearby or flung far.

As Waltner-Toews tells it, he was preparing to be a man of letters since boyhood. In 2012, he claimed his muse visited when he was a fervent youngster belonging to an ardent assembly, a Mennonite Brethren (MB) congregation to be specific, that "didn't really take poetry seriously as poetry," since it contains neither moral virtue nor financial value ("A Brotherly Philippic" 186). Elsewhere, Waltner-Toews explicated some of the Anabaptist convictions of his congregation. Devout "emphasis on mutual caring and correction, confessing to one another, and the community of believers" led Mennonites to value "practical ethics and plain speaking," so "[a]rtistic expressions were frowned upon; writers were liars and rascals; painters were on the slippery slope to ideology" ("Conversations" 162). In "'A Brotherly Philippic' to Tante Tina to the Mysteries of Disease, Death, and Transformation," Waltner-Toews conveys how falling for poetry hastened his descent to the ostensibly fallen world of the creative arts: "My grade 5 teacher, in a stroke of genius or extreme frustration, asked me to write a poem as punishment for talking in class" (186). The product of such unorthodox classroom management pleased his teacher so well it was published, as he relates in his Afterword in this book. Since childhood, Waltner-Toews has been writing for a community that is skeptical of poetry yet has nevertheless rewarded his forays into personal expression.

At age 12, Waltner-Toews and Hildi Froese Tiessen chummed around in the locker-lined halls of the Mennonite Brethren Collegiate Institute. Neither could know life would lead them to parallel professions in higher education—both would become authors and professors. Some sixty years after their initial encounter, Froese Tiessen honoured Waltner-Toews with an essay titled "Portrait of an Epidemiologist as a Young Man." Froese Tiessen's profile of her double-surnamed, thrice-credentialed friend and colleague begins with the Mennonite Brethren:

> a group of fairly progressive . . . congregations that were, when David and I were growing up, governed by rather rigid beliefs (some would prefer to say 'dogmas') about Christian salvation and discipleship and church protocols.

The two maintained contact after high-school graduation, and at one point she served as his *de facto* literary agent when he moved to Indonesia to work as an epidemiologist. In 1995, she interviewed him while researching the diaspora of Mennonite literature. He replied at length to her questions about the intersection between his poetic and scientific work:

> I struggled with how one might integrate the two . . . The language of literature, which valued ambiguity and harmonic resonance, was completely at odds with the language of academic scholarship, particularly

science, for which precision and perfect pitch were the highest values. From the start I tried to bring them together, if only for my own sanity. ("Portrait of an Epidemiologist")

It occurs to me that one could replace "academic scholarship, particularly science" with "religious inheritance, specifically Mennonite." As a result of these struggles, Waltner-Toews determined to treat his relationship with science similarly to the way he relates to his faith. Froese Tiessen pursued that line of questioning and drew this revelation from her subject: "Somebody once asked me why didn't I write more poetry with scientific language. It just seemed puzzling to me as to why one would write poetry with scientific language. It would kill the poetry" ("Portrait"). Rather than incorporating the detached style of academic scholarship into his poetry, he composed vernacular poems that comment on his life as a husband, father, and researcher. Writing along those lines, Waltner-Toews renders his "beliefs, science, and humanity" ("A Brotherly Philippic" 197) meaningful to both his communities, each in their own way pragmatic.

TRAVELOGUE

In the autumn of 1981, Waltner-Toews joined poet Patrick Friesen for an interview with Margaret Loewen Reimer and Paul Gerard Tiessen. At the time, Friesen was a little further into his writing career than Waltner-Toews, but both relate aspects of their personalities by revealing parts of their process. When asked who inspired his interest in poetry, Waltner-Toews names Mary Eleanor Bender, a professor at Goshen College, before digressing to say "I wanted to be a missionary cowboy when I was a child. That was my ambition" (246). In reply, Friesen quips that he once yearned to be a "missionary mountie." Waltner-Toews adds, "I grew up with a great feeling of pretension," adding "[t]here was always a very strong tendency among Mennonites to be self-righteous. I see that in my own writing and so I tend to back off and play the jester, right?" (247). He then becomes self-conscious about that anecdote: "But at this point I feel a little uncomfortable and I sometimes feel I'm still not taking my writing as seriously as I should." Such wisecracking and backtracking functions as an introduction, however unusual, to the poems he writes about travelling.

Although he never served as a missionary cowboy, Waltner-Toews grew up to be the next best thing—a travelling epidemiologist. His hyphenated surnames (he was born a Toews and added his wife's name after their marriage) were inscribed on an office door plate at the University of Guelph for 24 years, sure, but research took him around the world. Most of the resulting travel poems are sober-minded, which is striking for a poet known to possess an outlandish sense of humour. That may be because Waltner-Toews's research into zoonoses concentrates on infectious diseases spread between animals and humans, and so these poems describe how humans negotiate the natural world, both as individuals and as a community.

Whereas most tourists snap photos, Waltner-Toews jots poems. "Confessions of a Tourist Without a Camera" from the chapbook *The Earth is One Body* (1979) surreptitiously captures a moment in Point-à-Pitre, Guadeloupe from 1970. The speaker describes what he sees on vacation in the Caribbean, detailing how the faces of foreigners are obscured by camera lenses in order "to capture some of that mysterious vitality, / to make it theirs, to become it." Such an assimilative act is worrisome as it implies these tourists are not observing their surroundings so much as consuming them. Aboard "a touring ship rocking gently at dusk," they ignore the "sludgy water from the sugar cane factory" in favour of the local dance troupe pleasing them by "laughing, drumming into the bar-room circus ring." Waltner-Toews practices a comparable type of observation in a poem from the collection *The Fat Lady Struck Dumb* (2000) titled "Beached." With this snapshot, the first-person speaker reveals his discomfort amid other tourists relaxing on an unnamed beach:

> The sun on my skin
> is dry-ness. Is death.
> This body is made
> for water.

The speaker is beached in the sense that he feels isolated while lying belly down in the sand with waves lapping against his body. Breathing along with the aquatic rhythm, he longs to be fully absorbed into a unifying element of nature.

A trip to Java moved Waltner-Toews to write "Still Life, With a Mango," from *Endangered Species* (1988). With feet buried in white sand during "the heat of a Javanese afternoon," the speaker slices a mango and observes "its flesh is firm and wet / inviting the intrusion of a tongue." With the next line, he identifies with the open fruit:

It is the ocean on my body
after too much sun
the large wet hand of a wave
slipping down my limbs

In an unexpectedly erotic turn, evoking imagery from the Song of Solomon, the speaker remarks that the mango possesses a "swelling rounded body / firm giving slightly to the squeeze," including a "stiff nipple where the stem was" that "reminds me of something." The taste of "juice and happiness" leaves the speaker with "[t]he stone of a mango" and memories of "love's secret." While considering the fruit, life becomes as still as possible: "I hold it in my hand / I am satisfied."

Two poems that appear back-to-back in *The Fat Lady Struck Dumb*, "Death of a Humanist" and "Death of a Naturalist," present a captivating call and response about the effects of humanity on the natural world. Writing from Cortina, Italy, the speaker of "Humanist" enters "the chapel of La Faloria convent" where he pauses to consider some people who have previously stood where he now stands. After meditating upon Leonardo's "The Last Supper" in Milan, he seizes on "a wild and fragile thought" that seems to be "reaching out from between the cracks / in an aqueduct, or a cathedral / touching to reach me." By the end of the poem, he ponders why he feels close to the people who shaped the surroundings, even though he will never know them. Writing from Pugwash, Nova Scotia, the lyrical speaker of "Naturalist" pauses at dusk as "[t]he rising sea laps at my toes, / sucks at my heels." He dreams until dawn of travelling to Kathmandu and Kenya, India and Peru, and Honduras. From his subconscious a place surfaces "where life does not require its end / to live again, where passion has no price, / (such thin, immortal poverty of soul!)." After a night turning an ear to "sea-tongues" from "outside our cabin" singing "of love and death," the speaker wonders whether the death of the naturalist precedes the birth of the absurdist, or the surrealist, or maybe the expressionist. Curiously, in Seamus Heaney's poem of the same name, the speaker reflects on losing the love of nature he knew in his youth. In response, Waltner-Toews regards how the environment defies his attempts to capture it on the page.

A DIGRESSION INTO NATURAL CONVERSATION

I want to start the rumour that Waltner-Toews believes all flora and fauna are fluent in human language, but only the truly enlightened can hear them speak. Just look at his poetry about the natural world—it is almost as though he's trying to initiate dialogue. Just try to resist responding after reading the four lines below from a poem originally titled "Conversations with Nature." In the revised poem, entitled "Milton Hikes the Bruce Trail," the speaker, as its title would suggest, ponders the cosmogony of *Paradise Lost* while traversing a swath of rural Southwestern Ontario. The original version poses three rhetorical questions in a stanza about urinating next to a rattlesnake:

> Who really wrote
> those tales of deception and the Fall?
> Was Moses a urologist?
> And Freud, was he a herpetologist?

After briefly comparing his "pizzle" to "the snake's sleek, muscled coils," he contemplates "an empire of belonging lost." The speaker then questions whether Moses was learned in the ways of the male urinary tract, and whether Freud, the man who interpreted the book of Genesis in terms of collective guilt, knew his way around reptilian physiology. The four lines above do not appear in "Milton Hikes the Bruce Trail" as published in *The Gravity of Love* (2023). In both versions of the poem, the speaker ends the stanza by wishing he'd "gone back / to talk it over with the snake, / just brother to brother, guy talk" about "how our minds conquered, / how we lost the earth." The "Conversations with Nature" version makes it clear that we should question the anthropocentric assumption that humans possess knowledge unique to our being in the world.

In "Milton Hikes the Bruce Trail," the stanza in question no longer contains any reference to the biblical prophet or the father of psychology. In other words, Waltner-Toews has deleted any reference to the humans named in the poem. Instead, the speaker engages with those creatures he can identify by binomial nomenclature: a *Lepus americanus* (snowshoe hare), a *Crotalus horridus* (rattlesnake), and a *Tamias striatus* (eastern chipmunk) that he nicknames, as you might expect, "Tammy." In addition to such *Animalia*, the speaker also personifies members of the kingdom *Plantae* because aspens, junipers, and maples serve as avatars for a numinous idea of presence. The natural world, *contra* John Milton, does not require a fall from grace to develop an awareness that actions have consequences. When the speaker opens his mouth near the end of the poem to "pronounce some pithy epitaph," he longs for "a wash of wind / rushing and splashing" to redirect his mind toward "the waves on the lakeshore, / kissing the shore pebbles."

Still, and I get that my interpretation is probably idiosyncratic, I cannot shake the feeling that "Milton Hikes the Bruce Trail" is somehow incomplete. I am reminded of Roland Barthes' *Camera Lucida*, in which he posits that a photo is only a snapshot of an event or occurrence, and that the camera's subject will never be seen as whole. What's more, no two people will ever see the same photo in the same way: "A photograph's *punctum* [or small, distinct point] is that accident which pricks me (but also bruises me, is poignant to me)" (27). Oddly, the detail that provokes such a response may not even be intentional: the "*punctum* is also: sting, speck, cut, little hole—and also a cast of the dice." With those words, Barthes describes a subjective experience which others can't share. In effect, my understanding of the two versions of the poem is creating an individualized experience in that I'm reading my response into the text.

Because this interpretation is entering headlong into the domain of affect theory, I'll turn to two affect theorists for help. In their book *The Hundreds*, Lauren Berlant and Kathleen Stewart write brief reflections on "encounters with the world" that "are not events of knowing, units of anything, revelations or realness, or facts," and they call these instances "ordinaries" (5). With reference to Barthes, Berlant and Stewart describe how "'Punctum' ought to mean whatever grabs you into an elsewhere of form." This calls to my mind the missing lines from "Conversations with Nature," although readers who haven't slipped on white cotton gloves to visit archival files marked "David Waltner-Toews fonds" will have a different experience than mine.

One feature of Berlant and Stewart's way of thinking could apply to "Milton Hikes the Bruce Trail":

> There ought also to be a word like '*animum*,' meaning what makes an impact so live that its very action shifts around the qualities of things that have and haven't yet been encountered. You can never know what is forgotten or remembered. Even dormancy is a kind of action in relation. (5)

Following Berlant and Stewart, animum helps explain both the experience of reading "Milton Hikes the Bruce Trail" and the speaker's examination of relieving himself within the poem. Although I've never traversed the Niagara Escarpment, "Milton Hikes the Bruce Trail" animates a moment of reflection not unlike the one experienced by the poem's speaker. Whether or not the speaker actually squats at the water's edge by the poem's end to kiss tiny rocks, he ponders the possibility that he doesn't know all there is to know about the experience. In a way, the ambivalence in that encounter impacts my interpretation—I can sense myself as a stupefied member of *Animalia* among *Plantae*—because I remain aware that there is much more to be known about the qualities of these things.

FLORA

Waltner-Toews's work often constitutes a field guide that points out vegetation which readers must not miss. What's more, he seeds Latin terminology into several poems so we might observe *Plantae* anew. In "Identifying a Tree in the Fall" from *Endangered Species*, the first poem of what I affectionately term the tree triptych, the lyric speaker leads readers around the out of doors. He encourages us to crouch beside a tree to

See how it is rooted
among shrubs and boulders
Often you will see it thus
salmon-coloured gnarled bark
bending upward quivering
into a red crown

Although the speaker would have us envision the tree in question, he describes it in terms of what it is not. It is not like "the red maple" because "this tree loves darkness"; it is not like "the bent jack pine" because "this seeks out warmth"; it is not like "the mushroom" because "this flowers in a startling / burst of white blossoms." Waltner-Toews plants images *via negativa* to nurture imagination. The poem concludes with the suggestion that "if you touch these roots gently / there," readers "will feel the seedling stir / again softly." By encouraging us so, the speaker plants generations of trees that will grow in the mind.

A short poem from *Good Housekeeping* (1983) titled "Sweeping," the second poem in my imagined tree triptych, places readers in the middle of a blizzard. The speaker presents one simile to explain the title—"the trees like stiff brooms / quivered / against grey clouds"—and another simile that explains the relationship between us and their surroundings—"like trees we stood / out in the swirling / snow." While trees are "compulsively tidying / the sky," the speaker sweeps readers into the poem by using the plural pronoun, suggesting that weather erases distances separating neighbours. It seems worth noting that when reading the poem aloud, the last lines play with words: "snow // sweeping" could be read as "snow's // weeping." With that pun in mind, it appears as though when the clouds get emotional, everyone bears the brunt of their feelings.

The final poem of my tree triptych, "Trees," from *The Gravity of Love*, compares the separate processes of milling lumber, salvaging wood, and crafting words. In part one, the first-person speaker takes readers back to a conversation shared with the union steward of the Canadian White Pine Sawmill in 1970s Vancouver. "He is thinking about workers," but "I am considering ecology" over the sound of sawing white pine, Douglas fir, and yellow cedar into lumber. The speaker takes the side of "mutual aid, trees, co-evolution" in the discussion because he feels close to the trees—so close he must remind himself "This is not family." The speaker then takes us to Cape Chin South in 2000. He notes how the "wooden furniture creaks, / falls silent," and in that moment, his thoughts drift to the roof above and the roots below. While sitting still, he notices the surrounding maple, aspen, and fir. But, when "walking / among the trees," he senses "their thoughtless, perfect love / that holds, / and lets me go." The speaker honours them with four lines written on paper made from wood fibres with a softwood pencil atop a hardwood table. Part three, "The craft," offers this rhyming envoi:

> Oh sacred grove, now wounded,
> what can requite thy worth?
>
> Word, grooved with caring hand to word,
> a craft to bear us, earth to earth.

With that rhetorical flourish, we see the depths of Waltner-Toews's affection for the woods.

The eponymous poem "Endangered Species" from that volume contrasts feelings of loss with the presence of organic life. In part one, "The Disappearance," the speaker's reflection uses second-person address: "When your friends leave / you are a shrub." As you remain motionless, your friends become comparable to a snake slithering off, a cat turning away, and a crow flying south, leaving you "not knowing / they will return." Part two, "The Sighting," finds the speaker alone "in a boat / on an unruffled lake." A "sploosh" calls attention to "a spray / of silver flowers trailing / silver rippling necklace rings," and specifically toward "an empty centre." Still feeling hollowed by friends who have left, he is "not sure / what I am remembering" when he spots two loons passing and "three little ones / paddling madly after." Finding his loss mirrored, the speaker experiences comfort that feelings are fleeting, but life persists over generations.

FAUNA

It should come as no surprise that a veterinarian-slash-epidemiologist tends to wax eloquent about the animal kingdom. Waltner-Toews populates the biosphere of his poems with vivid imagery of fauna. For instance, "November Light" from *Endangered Species* depicts creation emerging at the time when sunlight is waning. It begins not long after the harvest, when the "air tumbles with scents of apples / pumpkins freshly dug carrots potatoes / black earth" in anticipation of renewal. The moment lingers as evening overtakes day in the midwinter dark. One January day, when promise is rare, the speaker recalls a miracle:

> I remember without thinking the bright turmoil
> of that time   It is Eden
> within me   left   and forever
> returning

Those thoughts appear as "a gently cupped hand / a graceful ark of dream-torn creatures / poised forever on a cresting wave." Nature itself celebrates that creative act.

The speaker of "A Man Sits Naked" from *The Fat Lady Struck Dumb* begins the poem perched on a mountaintop, musing about how he got there, how humanity got here, and how nature got caught. Before descending,

> He feels solidarity
> with his species, at one
> with all living things
> back into the ancient mists before time,
> back to slimy things climbing
> through algae and equisetum
> up the shore to earth, stones, roots.

I'm guessing the anonymous man hopes readers will look up the Latin term *equisetum*, discover "horsetail," and marvel that it has been around for over 100 million years. In the next stanza, a "man sits naked / on a street corner" before police capture him in the name of "the laws of Culture." The poem ends as the man, appropriately attired, "recalls a fragile newborn baby, / held in his chapped hands" while "[h]e hears the gulls" and interprets them as "crying, crying, crying." Birth, in those lines, provides a memory that counters alienation.

A similar isolated feeling imbues the poem "Something is Missing" from *Endangered Species*. The poem begins with an inclusive declaration:

Our bodies are
the interslipping of a thousand fish
fins sensing almost touch
a thousand neural tips
in playful synchronicity

All these near connections convey a sense of camaraderie between living beings. "It calls for a poem / It begs for a net," the speaker contends, but his lines flop and flutter "into the deep / lost blue." Presumably, we all move in schools, participating in the same ecology, but each of us feels apart from others. Although reaching out does not guarantee contact, it is still meaningful to try as such gestures shape the community of which we are a part. With the final stanza, "the poet eats fish / sticks with ketchup," which he suggests is "something short / of a religious experience." What's missing here is an epiphany. Even though he fishes for inspiration, the speaker dines alone.

In *The Impossible Uprooting* (1995), the poem "Breaking Free the Whales" offers "On Loving Earth Not Wisely, But Too Well" as a subtitle. This intriguing reference to Shakespeare conjures Othello's tragic last words as the poem positions readers atop "the thick ice crust / creaking, bending under / the sheer weight of our dancing." Observing the arctic waters off Alaska from a ship, the speaker describes how whales trapped in ice are released "into the swell of open sea." Since there appears to be no immediate threat to the crew or travellers, the ominous subtitle may refer to us all. Waltner-Toews later described how the rescue mission was "massive, expensive, and probably, ultimately, detrimental to the wild population of whales," but it "made a great many people feel good about themselves" ("Author's Notes" 137). The poem's conclusion represents that contradiction with

this sight: their gentle laugh
like a spout like a flag unfurled
like a hand waving
as they crest a distant wave

The compound comparisons in those lines refer to the seacraft, but they also hint at a larger change in the environment. The speaker then senses "under us / the ice crackles," echoing the ominous tone of the subtitle. Like Othello, we have acted in ignorance despite our best intentions.

ON OCCASION

After reading the poems in this section of this volume, you may feel like sending Waltner-Toews an invitation to an upcoming rite of passage—christening, baptism, first communion, bar/bat mitzvah, quinceañera/o, rumspringa . . . you name it. If he attends, he just might celebrate the day with an ode. See, as Waltner-Toews admits in "A Brotherly Philippic," his observant Anabaptist upbringing caused him to believe "writing had to be useful," and poems written "for occasions—birthdays, funerals, anniversaries" are undeniably useful (187). In the acknowledgments of *The Fat Lady Struck Dumb*, Waltner-Toews mentions that many of "these poems were written for particular people, and read at specific occasions" (118). That's not to say these occasional poems can't speak to us all. Waltner-Toews puts it this way: "Not sure if a particular poem was written for you? If the poem fits, wear it." With the following, he venerates other writers, honours his parents, and cherishes his wife.

Over the course of his career, Waltner-Toews has taken many an opportunity to give peers their flowers. Three poems in particular pay homage to his fellow wordsmiths. Waltner-Toews's ode for contemplative poet Pier Giorgio Di Cicco, "A Poem for Giorgio" from *Endangered Species*, searches for its subject on "the street you walk along / after a rain, the concrete glistening / under the greenish glare of streetlights." Then again, the speaker is not walking a sidewalk so much as travelling through time: "This is the street from 1967 to wherever" that rolls out like "a kind of runway" and lifts off "deeper into the twentieth century." He awaits in a state of limbo, "between fear, inadequacy and, / what the hell, / eternal hope." Pulling a Godot, Di Cicco does not arrive, which is fine once the speaker finds that the search is the point. The poet Tom Wayman cameos between the lines of "The Poetry of Work," an ode collected in *Good Housekeeping*. In section one, "Retrospective," the speaker looks back to find "it is possible / to write poetry / about the worst of jobs" like milling wood or jackhammering concrete. Wayman, the poet laureate of blue-collar labour, has built a career writing about jobs of that sort. The second section of "The Poetry of Work" starts with the speaker elbow-deep in a cow's rectum, wondering how serving as a veterinarian compares with his earlier work. The poem concludes by opining "[i]n another ten years / I may find this poetic."

Waltner-Toews dedicates "Roots," a poem which first appeared in *Good Housekeeping*, to a Mennonite contemporary. (He originally published the poem without any dedication, but the republished version is "not about Rudy Wiebe, but for him.") The poem begins with Wiebe tracing his genealogy while shovelling prairie soil: "He has roots on the brain. / He is looking for his roots." Although he doesn't find what he's looking for, he disinters "a dry bone" with a mysterious provenance and curious purpose:

> Rudy Wiebe cannot tell for sure
> what kind of bone it is.
> He watches the bone walk out to the road
> and head toward town.

In *Making Believe: Questions About Mennonites and Art*, Magdalene Redekop reflects on the implications of that reanimated bone. For Redekop, it represents "the Russländer narrative," a "tragic arc" of movement and loss (188). Waltner-Toews's "Roots" ploughs that soil, "breaking it up and releasing meaning on other levels" so that readers interrogate the history of Russian-Mennonite settlement in North America.

After long hours toiling in the garden, Wiebe calls it a day. Even after witnessing that miracle of the relic, "he still hasn't found any roots," so he "trudges home / bone in hand." When his mother greets him, he makes this concession: "Maybe you are right. Maybe my roots are in Russia." The two sit down over a bowl of "potato soup / with a bone in it," and Mrs.

Wiebe says that "[w]hen I was a girl in Russia . . . we ate this all the time." While contemplating "Roots" in his essay "The Mennonite Thing," Robert Zacharias explains how Waltner-Toews "raises the most conventional markers of Mennonite ethnic identity" by simultaneously "establishing a distance from the material even as he engages with it sympathetically" (118). Ironically self-reflexive, "Roots" solidifies "the very form of identity that it is ostensibly interrogating." Such "inversion of identity" applies to Waltner-Toews's writing practice itself. Regardless of what he writes, whether explicitly referring to his Mennonite inheritance or not, Waltner-Toews digs through layers of the past to understand who he is and where he comes from.

In addition, Waltner-Toews writes poems about events the rest of us would calligraph in the back of the leather-bound family Bible. For instance, he memorializes his father and mother with several poems. "Emmanuel" from *Good Housekeeping* mulls over "the presence of my dead father" while questioning the notion of a divine plan. Even the thought of eternity in paradise with "my dark forsaken God" offers "no consolation" to the speaker. Envisioning "volcanic ruptures" and "skies split by lightning and the thunderous / toppling of heaven's gilded pillars" provides "the only comfort," cold as it is. That theme of sincere grief extends to "The Door," also from *Good Housekeeping*. The speaker begins by connecting his father's rapport with horses with his father's later relationships with fellow church members. But then, "[h]e was gone," and the speaker is left to wander around a world without comfort. The poem concludes with a nod to Ecclesiastes, "[a]ll words are vanity." And, like the Preacher from that Old Testament scripture, the speaker knows how linguistic expressions are "all in vain"—still "[i]n the end, the door opens / Someone is there a guide perhaps." The poem does not identify the guide, but hopefully that unknown escort knows a little something about life and how to live it.

The lyric poem "On the Death of a Father" from *The Fat Lady Struck Dumb* is as honest an expression of grief as I've ever read. Using the second-person point of view, the speaker tries to come to terms with his father's passing:

You are left
alone
at the bottom of the sky,
at your doorstep.
At the foot of the stairs
you see him, turning.
He smiles.

As in "The Door," here the capacity for language to encapsulate grief is suspect: "There are no letters. / There is no word." The speaker of "On the Death of a Father" cannot stop to mourn because daily duties need attending to. "There is no pause," he notes; "You are already in the kitchen / peeling carrots / for lunch." After reading this mournful poem the article "a" of its title makes sense: the experience of the poem is not limited, but sadly universal.

The theme of inarticulate silence is similarly present in Waltner-Toews's poems about his mother. In "The Gift," a poem from *Endangered Species* with the dedication "for Mother . . . on her 75th birthday," the speaker pays tribute to a woman who survived being "reduced to the bone's / terrible whisper" in "a house abandoned." The poem is less about the effects of aging, than observing "the rich opaquely buffed layers / of your life   like a pearl before us." Even this "recollection," even this "remembering of / remembrance / will pass," but "the heart which we inherit" endures. In the ode composed after his mother suffered a heart attack, Waltner-Toews pays tribute to someone who "has seen it all, / from the Czar to Stalin, / Manning and Vander Zalm." According to the lyrical speaker of "My Mother's Heart Attack" from *The Fat Lady Struck Dumb*, such adversity is "all the same," whether it be personal or general:

Your husband dies.
Your children grow up.
Floods and famines,
politicians, families,
accountants, visionaries:
there is nothing new under the sun.

As in "The Door," Waltner-Toews channels the Preacher of Ecclesiastes when contemplating emptiness. The speaker confesses "All I can think of is my mother, / her silence, my tongue," but from that mouth "the twisted syntax / of my mother tongue / now from my lips is falling." The hope that might emerge from sorrow is entrusted to the reader.

After reading the poetry Waltner-Toews composed for his wife, I'm captivated by the maturity of their relationship. Their love is grown up, but that doesn't mean it's staid or solemn. The speaker of "The Next Ten Years" proposes being "messy lovers / drunk before breakfast." Waltner-Toews dedicates those lines to "Kathy," as "a tenth anniversary poem." The speaker characterizes their love in terms of "beans / O love we have spilled them," and personifies their shared secrets as legumes sprouting running feet and hands "clutching a spray of white flowers." In "Natural Love," the speaker returns to the idea of maturity by positing what love is not before settling into what it is. Love cannot be found "in clouds," "in soil," "in air," or "in cats"—"even the tomatoes" cannot produce love. The lyrical speaker calls forth love

> for nowhere is love writ but where your tongue
> inscribes, and nowhere read but where your lingering
> fingers tread the braille, and all that nature knows
>
> is scripted by the tussle
> of our bodies' calligraphic brush.

Love isn't found in things so much as the interpretation of things. Things can convey affection or charity, but natural love prospers through care and attention.

DOMESTICITY

The man of the house, according to Waltner-Toews, means literally that: the man's place is in the home. In his poems about domesticity, which I take to be voiced by males, speakers feel equally at home testing samples in the lab as they do crushing garlic in the kitchen. In his essay "The Practice of

Spirit," Waltner-Toews discloses that poetry "for me, is a way to converse with my experience of raw, complex reality"; it's "a way of . . . speaking to the deep Spirit of cow dung and snotty babies, of arguing with her [that deep Spirit] . . . until finally, she comes and I awake, exhausted, nervous, and full of hope, for another day" (72). Such a profound spiritual encounter can explain why he portrays the household as the centre of all good things. Nothing is quotidian there because everything matters more than it would initially appear.

In *The Earth is One Body*, Waltner-Toews sets the template for his domestic poetry with the short lyric "Homestead." The poem opens with the speaker declaring "I built this place" from "strong / green words." Then he offers readers a seat:

> I have been waiting for you
> here, beside the fire,
> between the lines,
> cords of unused words
> stacked up around me.

This action is not simply hospitality, it is also survival. The speaker has stored enough words to share when the nights get long: "I've left enough unsaid / to keep us warm / all winter." Having established the blueprint for a *poem*stead, if you will, Waltner-Toews builds another sort of community with "A Bill from the Power Company" from *The Fat Lady Struck Dumb*. This poem spans recorded history, with a scope as wide as imaginable. It starts with a stanza set in ancient New Guinea, where early humans contracted the neurological disorder Kuru, moves to the ramifications of cattle ranching in dustbowl America, and proceeds to the greedy 80s, where we see the effects of rabies and AIDS. The final stanza, though, focuses on two people who begin with "flowers and wine" and "clever conversation," and then express "the love of children, / of making them, and, surprisingly, caring for them." Such a community fulfills the promise of human civilization, with people "huddling by a campfire / playing old guitars, / singing plaintive melodies" to comfort themselves amid "the ash-black darkness."

In contrast to that depiction of communal life, Waltner-Toews describes the family life of a raptor in "Bird of Prey" from *The Impossible Uprooting*. Speaking though the beak of an anthropomorphised carnivore, Waltner-Toews compares the hunting and gathering practices of man and beast. The speaker begins by questioning its identity: "am I a white male? / was my first language German? / is this all my fault?" After establishing a link between animals at the top of the food chain, the speaker returns home with a small, brown mouse in its clutches. As the poem ends, the speaker confesses that "[t]he perfect two-kid two-car TV CD green lawn predator / I once despised / I have become." Talking with a man's tongue, the raptor resigns itself to its liminal place, neither grounded nor in flight: "There is no place to be / but here. / This is the story of my life." Having fallen prey to this malaise, the speaker seems to accept this dilemma, scarcely able to imagine an alternative.

The motivation for many of these domestic poems is providing for a family. In "The True Meaning of Being a Man," Waltner-Toews strives to thematically rhyme domesticity and masculinity. The speaker in this poem from *The Earth is One Body* gets so carried away rhapsodizing about the onions he's cutting for borscht that he drops too many in the pot. He begins by squeezing an onion "firm as a bulging bicep" before narrating how the muscular vegetable is the "colour of old ivory / smooth and sure as a man's career." After removing the first layer, the speaker finds the onion interior is "whiter, more vulnerable / than the last." Two layers in, he holds a bulb "delicate and lopsided / as a lover's balls." Before considering whether he has gelded the plant, the speaker ponders the "odour of this flesh, pungent as acid" that can provoke tears. His attention then turns to his own physique, "eyes gleaming / drenched in manful sweat." As he lowers the knife for one final cut, his wife intervenes by asking "Aren't you putting a lot of onions in the borscht?" After such a near-miss Freudian castration, the poem's title becomes clear. The true meaning of being a man is being strong enough to scrutinize the self.

No matter how often I've reread "Sunday Morning" from *The Fat Lady Struck Dumb*, I remain unsure what to make of the Crow figure. The poem seems to narrate the view out the windshield on the drive to church, only, as you might imagine, it is not quite so simple. At first, it's notable that the poem shares a title with a poem by Wallace Stevens. Whereas Stevens searches for morality to replace his childhood religion, Waltner-Toews questions how to best present his spiritual beliefs to his children. Whereas Stevens speaks of an aged woman in the poem, possibly as a ploy to explore the "holy hush of ancient sacrifice" (line 5), Waltner-Toews describes a father who grasps for words to describe the significance of faith. And, whereas Stevens refers to "casual flocks of pigeons" circling above, Waltner-Toews calls to Crow.

Waltner-Toews capitalizes Crow—a proper noun freighted with mythopoetic possibilities. The speaker observes Crow beside the highway and sees it as "a priest in black satin / casting his censorious beak / this way and that." He assumes this corvid of the cloth is awaiting a meal of roadkill or maybe some company to chat with. While Crow lingers outside, the speaker enters the sanctuary to sing with the congregation and listen to a sermon from the "woman at the pulpit, / black hair spread back / like raven's wings." And here we pause to consider why the preacher has the air of Crow. What are we witnessing? A prophetic warning? A trickster's ruse? Upon hearing of "bodies and boundaries, / the body of Christ, / the consummating heat of God," the speaker feels "lifted up / into a brave new heaven" where he is "above, finally, / all that history." Freed from the weight of the past, he perceives "the long silent night / surrounding us: / this is how the world ends." With that nod to "The Hollow Men," Waltner-Toews counters T.S. Eliot by contemplating the redemptive possibilities of participation in a religious community. The speaker leaves the service after observing "a small act of kindness," and with his family in the car, he spots "Crow in the rear-view mirror / anxiously waiting by the empty highway."

The revelatory moment from "Sunday Morning" recalls the scene between father and son in "Generations" from *Endangered Species*. The poem opens with the seven-year-old Matthew telling his dad, the first-person speaker, "that every day another species / disappears." As the speaker tucks his child into bed, their conversation turns from that degradation of nature to the transformation of a child's toy. Matthew requests "for next Christmas / a real Transformer" because he got a "Decepticon" last year. The speaker seizes on this "parable" of good versus evil, and considers "where else do our children dwell / but in the heavens / hells we think for them?" Next, the speaker comments that thinking in terms of oppositions is not inherent but inherited. "This is the essence is it not of *minding* children?" he asks. He responds sincerely with the declaration, "I feel myself coming loose." Matthew reappears in the ballad "The Snow Fort" from *The Impossible Uprooting*, but this time his sister Rebecca joins. The speaker starts by saying "[o]nce a year we built a fort," piling "the chunks / of uneven, prickly ice" until he and the children disappear. The three then march out from their makeshift shelter over "misty snowbound peaks / and hummed Amazing Grace," only returning home

> if the sky fell down
> and bonked us on the head
> or someone was calling Dinner Time!
> or our toes felt like cold lead.

The poem ends by repeating the first stanza as a sort of hymn sing. Such repetition evokes the cycles of parenthood, and domesticity itself. Time passes, but there are no ordinary hours.

A DIGRESSION INTO TANTE TINA'S TALK

Where I come from, everybody has at least one auntie Tina. The poems that Waltner-Toews composed in the voice of the elderly Mennonite lady with that name sound uncannily like some Tantes I know. Although Tante Tina makes no claim to being a poet—she's just making conversation, after all—she has a recognizable way with words. And over forty years of writing as Tina, Waltner-Toews has honed her voice by revising several poems after their initial publication. And even subtle changes, a Froese here, a line Enns there (regardless of Reimer reason), can significantly affect their vocal tone. Closely reading the alterations that Waltner-Toews made to "Tante Tina's Lament" will reveal some important traits of his persona.

In "Tante Tina's Lament," one of the earliest dramatic monologues, the titular speaker bewails the fact that her son Hänschen has moved to Winnipeg. However, the implied audience for her lamentation is never clear. At first, Tina appears to address her husband Doft, but he must already be abreast of her feelings about Hänschen's goings-on; why tell him something he already knows? At the end of the poem, the audience changes as Tina implores "my son" to "come home." She promises "I will make you porzelky for breakfast / and we will celebrate the New Year / every morning." Given the work involved in deep frying New Year's cookies, Tina must be desperate to coax her prodigal son. So, is she apostrophizing Hänschen? Is she rending her garments and shouting at passersby? Could she be praying even?

The original version of "Tante Tina's Lament" that appears in *Good Housekeeping* opens with a simile describing how "Hänschen struts about the city / like a chicken." Tina objects to the galling threads her son wears about town, a "pink shirt / and plaid, big-bottomed hosen." Tina ends the first stanza by teasing that, in truth, her son has shown such *galline* tendencies since he was small, as when "I spanked his little buns / and how he crowed!" The poem reappears in *The Impossible Uprooting*, but two telling alterations have been made in spelling and syntax: 1) the umlaut in "Hänschen" has been replaced with the "ae" ligature; and 2) subject-verb-object word order has been revised with an idiomatic subject-object-verb construction. The first adjustment is likely only stylistic, but it does speak to how Russian-Mennonite surnames were anglicized while immigrating to North America. The second, though, signifies a shift in Tante Tina's characterization. The newer "Lament" establishes that "Haenschen in the city / struts, like a chicken." Waltner-Toews has changed the location of the verb in an idiosyncratic *Plautdietsch*, or Low German, move. Moreover, he breaks the line before the verb, emphasizing this structure, atypical in English but not in Low German. The first stanza concludes with a similar change, placing the verb after the object: "His little buns I spanked / and how he crowed!" Later in the poem, Waltner-Toews swaps "Now he wags his tongue at me" with "Now his tongue he wags at me," while "I don't know how to barbecue a steak" becomes "I a steak don't know how to barbecue." Most egregiously, "They eat platz and give testimonies" now reads "They are platz eating and testimonies giving." There other examples are, but I my point have made.

Plautdietsch is Tante Tina's mother tongue, so the word order in the original "Lament" does not hit the Mennonite ear quite right. To this reader raised near Altona, Manitoba (just about the place where Tante Tina resides), the syntax of the revised poem sounds more familiar. Like

Hänschen, my parents are Low German speakers, but I speak not the dialect myself. Magdalene Redekop, by contrast, is fluent in *Plautdietsch*, and in *Making Believe*, she makes an intriguing observation about "Waltner-Toews and his way of mixing up English, High German, and Low German in the voice of Tante Tina" (197). "I deduce," Redekop continues, "that Waltner-Toews did not speak Low German growing up, from the fact that he writes *Tante* instead of *Taunte*." Sure enough, when I see "Tante" on the page, the latter pronunciation comes to mind. Redekop suggests that Waltner-Toews is "searching for a connection with his mother tongue" (197), and, honestly, she could be talking about me as well. I'll add that the *Plautdietsch* in "Lament" presents an opportunity to readers to feel a part of a community. In other words, Tante Tina talks that way to remind Hänschen about the meaning of home.

Even though I feel a pang of homesickness while reading "Tante Tina's Lament," the language also seems inherently funny. The syntax, for instance, calls to mind the idiom "what it not all gives?" that is still heard around the Manitoba Mennonite "West Reserve," and is roughly equivalent to "good heavens!" or "what on earth?" There is similarly exaggerated playful incredulity in "Tante Tina's Lament" when Tina notes that her son, her only begotten, "says Low German is a pile of manure." She promises to "surround you with Low German. / I will piles of it to you be speaking. / Then you will know what Low German is!" Redekop explicates this conceit as depicting "the class differences that separate High German from Low German" and English yet too (197). Redekop obviously knows what she's speaking about, but I read Low German in the poem as a complement to those other languages. For me, *Low* German does not imply class inferiority, but a dialect that's earthy, maybe crude, but also authentic and down to earth. In addition, Tante Tina uses a comedic style of rhetoric common among southern Manitoba Mennonites: hyperbole. If you ask Tina, Winnipeg is lousy with women of ill repute, unlike the inherently virtuous women from Altona. For instance, Hänschen's girlfriend on "her lips has red grease besmeared," so the young ladies of Altona appear more wholesome by contrast—especially since their "cheeks are rosy from harvest." Of course, Tina doesn't mean such a smear literally. Such humourous exaggeration lets her express fear and frustration without giving too much offence.

How do people without even a passing familiarity with *Plautdietsch* deal with all this? Hildi Froese Tiessen addresses that very issue in her influential essay "Mother Tongue as Shibboleth in the Literature of Canadian Mennonites." Simply put, "outsiders" do not engage easily, and that is the idea. The presence of Low German in English-language literature presents a deliberate challenge to readers:

> Whatever these authors hope to accomplish through their use of mother tongue, the result of their technique is to divide their audience into insider and outsider and so, in effect, to re-establish barriers separating the traditional Mennonites' experience from the world's. (69)

Plautdietsch offers a thick layer of itchy pink insulation against the influences of a hegemonic culture. It is a linguistic protest by a community that knows a thing or two about Protestantism. The Russian-Mennonite community Tante Tina belongs to is justifiably wary about assimilation, much like their Mennonite relations across Western Canada and the American Midwest. According to Froese Tiessen, one way to maintain a "separation from and nonconformity to the world" is by codifying "the ethos, the cultural and spiritual texture of a Mennonite world that no longer exists" (68). Of course, no matter how much work traditionally-minded Mennonites put into preserving Low German like pickled beets, its importance has diminished.

While reading Froese Tiessen's essay, I feel a tinge of regret because I was raised by parents who spoke a *Plautdietsch* and English patois when they did not want me or my siblings to catch onto what they were saying. And when "*Plaut*-lish" ("*Eng*-dietsch"?) circled the dinner table, we knew something was afoot. Desperate to crack the code, I recall trying to replicate the few words I recognized, but my tongue failed to wrap around the syllables. No matter how hard I tried, my mispronunciations and anglicized accent told on me. That sort of social phenomenon, according to Froese Tiessen, follows the logic of the "shibboleth," where something as simple as phrasing can distinguish one group from another. Froese Tiessen specifically refers to the end of "Tante Tina's Lament" to contend that an insider hears its language "as a kind of exclusive intertextuality that probes poignantly beyond the gentle humour of the poem into the last records of a people's fading means of common (and exclusive) discourse" (68). While the outsider may chuckle at an elderly Mennonite lady's embellishments, the insider's laughter could be covering up anxiety.

TANTE TINA TALKS

In *Making Believe*, Magdalene Redekop proposes that "Tante Tina talks back" to those with whom she takes issue, "and the reader is free to do so" in kind (222). I'll take up that reading to consider how it was Tante Tina began talking and how it is she prompts others to talk back. Waltner-Toews addresses the origin of his persona in the essay "A Brotherly Philippic" when he confesses that "at the age of 30, I had never written anything creative with the word 'Mennonite' in it" because that would have been hard to do "without stirring up all the anger and angst and cynicism that I associated with my MB upbringing." When Waltner-Toews later determined to speak to and about his cultural heritage, he quickly discovered a suitable tone: "since the real history of Mennonites was told by women in the kitchen and not by the historians in the library, the voice would need to be female." So, he channeled his mother and her sisters, "especially the strong-willed and outspoken Tante Truda, [who] were obvious choices" (194). The resulting "real Mennonite poems" appeared a year later in *Canadian Forum* to a receptive readership.

Waltner-Toews not only traces the familial lineage of Tante Tina, he also notes another important literary influence. He writes of his wife Kathy giving him a copy of Okot p'Bitek's epic poem *The Song of Lawino*, written "in Luo, a decidedly non-mainstream African language [that] was translated, warts and all, directly into English. He called his style 'comic singing'" ("A Brotherly Philippic" 194). Taking a page from *The Song of Lawino*, Waltner-Toews wrote Tante Tina as speaking idiomatic English. He asks himself "Did I appropriate that voice?" and answers in the contrary: "I would say she appropriated me" ("A Brotherly Philippic" 196). And he truly means that; on occasion Tante Tina possesses him. Waltner-Toews has performed as her many times over the years since her creation. Although his performance is ongoing, I hesitate to call that practice performative in the philosophical tradition of J.L. Austin through to Judith Butler. Waltner-Toews embodies Tante Tina, yes, but the performance is neither an "illocutionary act" (Austin 115)—a declaration, command, or promise that takes effect when spoken—nor "a stylized repetition of acts" that produces "the appearance of substance" (Butler 519). In a manner of speaking, Tante Tina lives on her creator's tongue.

Tante Tina will hold forth about whatever crosses her mind, but she tends to favour three topics: food, faith, and affairs of state. That said, regardless of what she speaks about, she usually brings it back to family. For instance, "Tante Tina Talks about Her Man" tells the story of Tina's relationship with Doft while also speaking to the centrality of the church. Tina first noticed Doft when he was praying with his brother Peeta; they married while in Bible School. Importantly, Tina couches farm labour in religious terms: "The more hard we worked / the more the Lord blessed." Since her poems usually are flavoured with irony, such sincerity demands our attention. Moreover, the reason Tina laments is not only for her son leaving home, but also for his forsaking of traditions that shaped him.

This is not to suggest that Tante Tina doesn't get through to Hänschen. Proof of her influence appears in "Hänschen's Success," where the son gets the final word for once. After moving to the city and swapping practical dungarees for fashionable corduroys, Hänschen exults in his newfound sartorial freedom with reference to Handel's *Messiah*:

> Now, when I the door swing open
> in the morning
> it's like a Hallelujah Chorus in cotton
> singing me out into the day

While epiphanizing, Hänschen also parodies another Handel composition, the hymn "As Pants the Hart," based on Psalm 42: "Thus, every day, scripture and my thighs / are fulfilled and I respond, 'Dear Lord, / my heart pants for thee." He plays the psalmist in the way his mother acts as deuteronomist in "Tante Tina Tells a Bible Story." In this poem, Tina describes how she hung onto the Bible and clung to its stories when emigrating to Canada. In particular, she kept one finger in the Book of Judges where Jael drove a tent peg into Sisera's temple and another finger in 2 Samuel where

David lusts after Bathsheba. At the end of the poem, Tante Tina considers how her family (and the Mennonite community overall) have colonized land in southern Manitoba: "In Canada, I have heard, the Indians are tents having. / So, I am thinking, they must tent pegs have. / A safe country. I am thinking. A safe country." Perhaps this country will only be safe for Indigenous people who wield tent pegs as camping supplies as well as weapons.

Although the small town of Altona may appear to be isolated from the world, Tante Tina would tend to suggest otherwise. She seems unusually versed in affairs of state, both inside and outside of Canadian borders. At first, she may seem confused about the finer points of socio-political intrigue in "Tante Tina Calls in to a Canadian Radio Talk Show." On second glance, however, she knows much more than she lets on. She purposefully confuses a few details, which allows her to align the 1983 American invasion of Grenada with the 1979 Russian invasion of Afghanistan—and by doing so she hints that the Mennonite immigration to Manitoba could also qualify as an invasion. Her solution is like others she has offered in these talks: "I think they should all come back / to Manitoba" and hash it out over a plate of home cooking. Tante Tina extends similar hospitality to Margaret Thatcher in "Tante Tina Reflects on Maggie Thatcher" where she suggests her baking (in this case a sweet loaf of bread and cottage cheesecakes) could inspire religious conversion. Tina compares Thatcher's reputation as the "Iron Lady" to "*geröstete Zwieback*," double buns baked too long. Instead of being pleasantly crunchy, Thatcher's crust is hard, so

> She needs dipping in some tea,
> get those buns wet already yet,
> a good immersion baptism, and then
> confession: *Lieben sie die Brueder?*

Does the Prime Minister love her brethren? Tante Tina can't say, but perhaps this ceremony will inspire Maggie to join the community of believers. After all, confession is good for the soul, and for saving it as well.

Tante Tina busies herself by airing fiery judgements and sharing folksy adages to keep her hands—hands that, like Waltner-Toews's own, both delivered calves and ladled borscht—from growing idle. When considering the work of someone as accomplished as Doctor-Professor-David, someone whose credentials range from scientific disciplines to the creative arts, all his fields of knowledge could never be adequately represented in a single text. So, here we are, sitting with a selection of his poems. This book isn't comprehensive or exhaustive, since it would be impossible for a book to encompass the variety of the subjects Waltner-Toews has written about. At the very least, this volume is a sample of a restless mind. And, by the end, its author, like Tante Tina herself, will have the last laugh.

Austin, J. L. *How to Do Things with Words*. Oxford University Press, 1962.

Barthes, Roland. *Camera Lucida: Reflections on Photography*, translated by Richard Howard, Hill and Wang, 1981.

Berlant, Lauren, and Kathleen Stewart. *The Hundreds*. Duke University Press, 2019.

Butler, Judith. "Performative Acts and Gender Constitution: An Essay in Phenomenology and Feminist Theory." *Theatre Journal*, vol. 40, no. 4, 1988, pp. 519–531.

Eliot, T.S. "The Hollow Men." *Poems: 1909–1925*. Faber & Gwyer, 1925, pp. 123–128.

Heaney, Seamus. "Death of a Naturalist." *Death of a Naturalist*. Faber & Faber, 1966, pp. 15–16.

Plett, Casey. *On Community*. Biblioasis, 2023.

Redekop, Magdalene. *Making Believe: Questions About Mennonites and Art*. University of Manitoba Press, 2020.

Reimer, Margaret Loewen, and Paul Gerard Tiessen. "The Poetry and Distemper of Patrick Friesen and David Waltner-Toews." *Visions and Realities: Essays, Poems, and Fiction Dealing with Mennonite Issues*, edited by Harry Loewen and Al Reimer, Hyperion Press, 1985, pp. 243–253.

Stevens, Wallace. "Sunday Morning." *Harmonium*. Knopf, 1923, pp. 100–104.

Tiessen, Hildi Froese. "Literary Refractions." *The Conrad Grebel Review*, vol. 20, no. 1, 2002, pp. 102–103.

---. "Mother Tongue as Shibboleth in the Literature of Canadian Mennonites." *On Mennonite/s Writing: Selected Essays*. CMU Press, 2003, pp. 61-70. Originally published in *Studies in Canadian Literature,* 1988.

---. "Portrait of an Epidemiologist as a Young Man: Reflections on the Poetic, Peripatetic Life/Lives of David Waltner-Toews." *Hamilton Arts & Letters,* vol. 13, no. 2, 2020–2021, https://samizdatpress.typepad.com/hal_magazine_thirteen-2/david-waltner-toews-by-hildi-froese-tiessen-1.html.

Waltner-Toews, David. "Author's Notes." *The Impossible Uprooting*. McClelland & Stewart, 1995.

---. "'A Brotherly Philippic' to Tante Tina to the Mysteries of Disease, Death, and Transformation: Mennonite Reflections on a Life of Poetry and Science." *Conrad Grebel Review,* no. 31, vol. 2, 2013, pp. 185–207.

---. "Conversations with the Dead." *Poetry as Liturgy: An Anthology by Canadian Poets,* edited by Margo Swiss, St. Thomas Poetry Series, 2007, pp. 161–175.

--- [@DoftWT]. "Shouldn't confuse 21st C human civilization with the world." Twitter, 30 Jun. 2019, https://x.com/DoftWT/status/1145344661717999616.

---. "Confessions of a Tourist Without a Camera," "Homestead," "The True Meaning of Being a Man." *The Earth is One Body,* Turnstone Press, 1979.

---. "Sweeping," "The Poetry of Work," "Roots," "Emmanuel," "The Door," "The Next Ten Years." *Good Housekeeping,* Turnstone Press, 1983.

---."Still Life, With a Mango," "Identifying a Tree in the Fall," "Endangered Species," "November Light," "Something is Missing," "A Poem for

Giorgio," "The Gift," "Generations." *Endangered Species*, Turnstone Press, 1988.

---. "Breaking Free the Whales," "Natural Love," "Bird of Prey," "The Snow Fort." *The Impossible Uprooting*, McClelland & Stewart, 1995.

---. "Beached," "Death of a Humanist," "Death of a Naturalist," "A Man Sits Naked," "On the Death of a Father," "My Mother's Heart Attack," "A Bill from the Power Company," "Sunday Morning." *The Fat Lady Struck Dumb*, Brick Books, 2000.

---. "Tante Tina's Lament," "Tante Tina Talks about Her Man," "Haenschen's Success," "Tante Tina Tells a Bible Story." *The Complete Tante Tina: Mennonite Blues and Recipes*, Pandora Press, 2004.

---. "Milton Hikes the Bruce Trail," "Trees." *The Gravity of Love*, St. Thomas Poetry Series, 2023.

---. "The Practice of Spirit." *Poetry and Spiritual Practice: Selections from Contemporary Canadian Poets*, edited by Susan McCaslin, St. Thomas Poetry Series, 2002, pp. 71–72.

---. "Falling in Love with Poetry: What's Love Got to Do with It?" *The New Quarterly*, vol. 99, 2006, https://tnq.ca/story/whats-love-got-to-do-with-it.

Zacharias, Robert. "The Mennonite Thing: Identity for a Post-Identity Age." *After Identity: Mennonite Writing in North America*, edited by Zacharias, University Manitoba Press, 2015, pp. 106–122.

This collection is dedicated to my Grade 5 teacher at Polson Elementary School in East Kildonan, whose name I cannot recall. She made me write a poem as punishment for talking in class and then praised the result. Since then, I have never been able to stop writing, searching to find again that exhilarating line between punishment and reward.

A Post-Cambrian Lament

Her feet sting
on the hot Namibian sand.

Far below, now cast in stone,
Cambrian worms once danced, engorged,
the spiny slug fantastique,
carnivorous exuberance . . . Ottoia,
Hallucigenia, Wiwaxia, Aysheaia . . .
limbs and tongues commingled
in a slice of time,
540 million years ago,
ten million wide.

Later, the Bushmen
brushed carefully their scenes of game,
their hunger,
and our insatiable desire
against these rocks:
the graceful leap of creatures
from veldt to stone to wavering
thin air.

From a multiplicity of shapes in species
to this polyphony of human voice:
filmmaker, archaeologist, farmer,
cacophonic symphony
of ecotourists, businessmen,
choir of utter poverty.

She stands still at the rim;
the valley falls away
before her.

This is the world's first breath,
its last breath, bated.
From the plunging sweep
below, a shimmering sigh of microbes
lifts, in expectation of great carnage,
an orgy feast across the landscape,
another brilliant efflorescence.

Her limbs strain, quivering slightly,
rooted, mesmerized by sand in wind,
a vision of our end
in hot reflected sun.

Travelogue

Beached

I focus on my breathing,
the full weight of all I have become
pressing gently, firmly down
against my ribs, the entering
and leaving of salt winds,
cries of sea birds
to my heart,
from all my heart.
The sun on my skin.

The sun on my skin
is dry-ness. Is death.
This body is made
for water.

I focus on the others
now, the young ones
slipping through the water,
water leaping ahead
of itself, its white ears flopping
ahead of itself, over the waves;
leaping into the air
they pass. The air is a challenge
for them, a thrill, a rush
of adrenalin. They
flute fountains. They fountain white
spitting hisses of joy.

If I make no sound
they will not see me.
If I cry
they will gather, they will mourn.
I will die seeing their sad eyes.

I want to die
full of ballet and bravado,
my mind a dance from water to air
to water, unthinking joy.

I make no sound, the wet
rock at my belly, the cool
water licking its slow
infinite sadness, the forgiveness of oceans,
the wisdom of heavy seas,
the sun at my back,
like a warm hand,
with each slowing breath
my spirits falling,

and rising.

Still Life, with a Mango

The swelling rounded body,
firm, giving slightly to the squeeze,
stiff nipple where the stem was,
reminds me of something.

As it rests in my hand
fresh, as from a bath,
I think of mountains in Java,
a wet-nosed stallion, muscular
but friendly, nibbling from my palm
before he canters along the breathless
inter-paddy paths to a waterfall.
Bright flowers hide like little children
aching to be found
among the green leaves.

When the mango is opened
its flesh is firm and wet
inviting the intrusion of a tongue.

It is the ocean on my body
after too much sun,
the large hand of a wave
slipping down my limbs.

The flesh of the mango is sweet and cool,
filling the heat of a Javanese afternoon
with juice and happiness.
The moment of its eating brims so full
there is no room for reflection.

The stone of a mango
is love's secret,
the heart's uncut diamond,
slippery with memories.

I hold it in my hand.
I am satisfied.

Confessions of a Tourist Without a Camera

The harbour at Point-à-Pitre, Guadeloupe:
sludgy water from the sugar cane factory
lapping at rotting wood;
a tourist ship rocking gently at dusk
like an old woman gently rocking on this back porch
of the Caribbean; she is an autumn ship
replete with wildlife of Manhattan
and Montreal, varicose-veined squirrels
and puffy-cheeked gophers
sipping Manhattans and Bloody Marys.
They carry their bellies, pregnant with excess retirement,
like flour sacks, smuggled out of America
under gay Hawaiian shirts;
breasts like overripe melons
sag in cheese cloth sacks;
legs in too-short shorts, like drumsticks at the grocery,
pale-skinned and goose-bumped.

The local dance troupe troops on board
laughing, drumming into the barroom circus ring,
lithe, black, gleaming with sweat,
swirling brightly coloured remnants,
grinning mouthfuls of polished ivory;
and I with them, a tourist of tourists,
writing pictures of the picture-takers.

One snap:
the sagging faces behind the cameras,
sad gopher eyes squinting through Minolta keyholes,
anxious hands, sweaty, fumbling with buttons
and knobs, wanting,
more than any gold watch or turkey banquet,
to capture some of that mysterious vitality,

to make it theirs, to become it.
Would they later, desperate in the face
of death's daily quiet advances,
eat the film?

I move into the shadows
down the wooden plank, through the deserted market,
warm streets, the moist and heavy night.
Young people are playing volleyball
in the town square.
Back in my room I slowly chew up the pages
on which my poems are written,
not to capture or become,
but to forget, to become innocent
again, to never have known the faces, the eyes, the hands.

Through my window
I can hear faint sounds of applause and laughter.

Death of a Humanist

In the chapel of La Faloria convent,
Cortina, Italy, I meditate
in the quiet dawn,
a shadow of habits
supplicating behind me,
before me the silhouette of a cross,
stark against the white mountain
and the Arian clear blue sky.

Later, I climb
a well-groomed mountain path
through the congregation of trees.
At the top there is a chapel, a guest house,
and a large military gun.
Up there, the sheer delight
of earth's power, barely constrained,
rolls like an organ fugue
down, away from me
into a complex canon of trills and rocks
and breathtaking valleys,
up, billowing like a ragged windblown sheet
into the vaulted skies.
It tugs, at every peak,
against the slipping grip
of guest house, chapel, gun.

Below, in Milan,
I walk the narrow streets,
feeling at home, pause in the courtyard
of the Giuseppe Verdi Music Conservatory
in the Chiesa della Passione (AD 1486).
Violin sounds dip and wing
from balconies,

musicians in formal attire
pace gracefully, humming.
Around a corner, the Duomo
rises in the Central Plaza,
from a distance like an intricate
wet-dripped sand castle.
Up close, it is a rock-heap
of men on horses, torsos rippling,
biceps bulging in triumph and misery,
swords, flags, crosses

upthrust in victory.

For a millennium these bodies
chopped, hauled, reorganized,
reshaped wood, stone, earth,
cut and slashed each other over differences
of opinion, convinced each other
with argument, praised God, made
God redundant with thumbscrews,
racks, irons, stakes,
proved that people were superior
to God in all these things, carved the Duomo
in stone dragged down from the Dolomites,
rebuilt the mountains
in our own image until wild snow,
rock canyons, fearsome beast,
were transformed to cathedral, sewer, hospital,
factory, guest house, gun.

I sit at the edge of the plaza,
security helicopters buzzing overhead,
brilliant lights enflaming the magnificence
of stone, eating pizza, drinking red wine.
I sense the full weight of it,

the mass of flesh screaming
through the centuries, raining
down on me, arms, legs,
bodies of knowledge,
corporate legacies
like a legion of mad prions remaking the earth
in our image, demanding rights, attention, liberty,
trampling every living thing in the pursuit
of truth, beauty,
and efficient management.

I close my eyes,
recalling the small, dusky space
where Leonardo depicted a gathering of twelve men
arguing during a meal, one,
lost in sadness, seeing too far ahead.
I imagine the possibility of unprovoked, unexplained
acts of wildness and love,
animals escaping, unfinished business,
finished business undone, half-fallen cathedrals
awhirr with the happy chat and clicks

of swallows and bats, and
scattered showers of light.

Something brushes my cheek
in the dark, gently,
a small, dry, green hand,
the touch of a wild and fragile thought, lost in the midst
of all this order, like a friend, remembered,
reaching out from between the cracks
in an aqueduct, or a cathedral,
touching to reach me.

I open my eyes.
A wind sweeps across the plaza,
the lights go out,
unsure lovers huddle slowly past.

I feel something
like hope. I hold it gently,
feel it scrabble and nip
in the chambers of my heart,
like a small bird, or a mouse caught
in the garden shed.

I let it go free in the dusk.

Death of a Naturalist

In the red-hued water
off Pugwash, Nova Scotia,
red jelly-coloured jellyfish
slip and waltz one over the other
to the shore. In the retreating tide
they sag into tangles of crocheted
seaweed, like fatigued dancers
into satin bedsheets.

What wild, colossal waste!
What brutish inefficiency!
What waves of beautiful recycling
tumbling over under one form to another
life unfolding rolling folding from sighing choirs
of plankton to waltzing fish to jitterbugging microbes
to clams with laidback erections
pushing up through the muck at my feet
to garlicked succulence in oil
to me. What would I feel
if the sea were casting human babies
up on the sand?
What do my feelings matter?

Out on the bay, a Right Whale and a Humpback
break the static-hiss of waves.
In clear, dark lines, they
graze the interface of vast unspeaking worlds,
raise cryptic messages,
slip under.
Waves of shore birds lift, turn and fall
like a grand musical score.
The rising sea laps at my toes,
sucks at my heels.

Somewhere inland, an aging porcupine
bids his friends a calm farewell.
Around them, choirs of flies hum distractedly;
the crows cannot restrain
their raucous glee.

I am retreating homeward, inland,
drawn by the pistons' fevered beat
through falling night, away
from nature's dark and brilliant
orchestration, drawn to four walls, a quilted bed,
my lover's arms, high-minded dreams
of some sad planet
where every death is wasted,
where life does not require its end
to live again, where passion has no price,
(such thin, immortal poverty of soul!)

where I could turn, relieved, from these, our sacrifice—
the street kids hassling me in Kathmandu
and Kenya, the girls bent over,
beating waves of cotton on the rocks in India
and Peru, the peasant farmers in Honduras
scratching chicken feed from mountain soil,
from spirits broken,
from hearts undone.

The porcupine waits on the road
raising, with slow dignity,
in the glare of inexorable lights,
his quivering crown. The driver
flinches
at the thump, but does not stop.

All night outside our cabin
the sea-tongues sing
of love and death,
of jellyfish and fishermen,
of whales and sailing watchers,
of diatoms, mud shrimp, sandpipers,
old porcupines, middle-aged poets,
laundry girls, street kids, farmers, coiling and recoiling,
arias, duets, and chorus after rich-voiced
chorus, echoing against sea-glass and sand
against shifting fossil-bearing shale.

As morning fog inexorably
brightens
in the harbour, I turn
to face the window
and drift
to sleep.

The Mind

A life cycle based on Dictyostelium discoideum, a slime mould,
which is sometimes a plant, and sometimes an animal

In the wake of sun's departure
the mind stirs   pulls up its roots
and scatters   The skull cannot hold
these amoeba They slink
to the corners of the backworld
to the compost heaps and yogurt tubs
of Everyday gone decadent

The mind feeds on these things
things of reverberating substance
matter transubstantiated into God
knows what   hyena's death-laugh   the crows'
scavenging craw   the impudent lifeburst of pollywogs
the momentary permanence of marigolds

This is not death
This is preparation   See
my grandfather is here   He will tell you
about teaching in the Ukraine   He knows
about the Revolution   He can explain
death   that perfection
of the mind's animal   a prowling
between stars   flicking
of tongues   fins and legs
in matter's resonance
innocence in love perfected

Death is not returning
from this nightplace not morning when
the mindslugs cringe into themselves

become a sorocarp on spine's stalk
nerve rootlets and a puff of dreamspores
and in the brittle sunrise
my self

Flora

November Light

Hesitant beside an opened cage door
we poise at birth
We cannot believe this is happening
this breathless ruffle
this life

The air tumbles with scents of apples
pumpkins freshly dug carrots potatoes
black earth   trembles with the unsung carol
of cedar waxwings amid sprigs of red berries
and the white sigh of snow-breasts

In this brief infinity of hesitation
lurks the fear of being caught of not catching
blooms the flower
of forever-being-lost
the broken tongue's rough-stemmed bitterness

And as Fall sunlight
leafs between the trees' thorned crowns
we dance
like cats following birds in teasing leaps
we weave between the still trees circling
in the dance of tyrants' toppling
the dance of childhood
of almost catching almost being caught
catbird oneness trailing bright threads
encasing ourselves this moment
in a cocoon of pure light

On January's muffled dark sea
I remember without thinking the bright turmoil
of that time   It is Eden

within me   left   and forever
returning   a gently cupped hand
a graceful ark of dreamtorn creatures
poised forever on a cresting wave

just above the ragged contours
of the inevitable reef

Identifying a Tree in the Fall

See how it is rooted
among shrubs and boulders
Often you will see it thus
salmon-coloured gnarled bark
bending upward quivering
into a red crown

Unlike for instance the red maple
this tree loves darkness
Unlike the bent jack pine
this seeks out warmth
Unlike even its own metaphor the mushroom
this flowers in a startling
burst of white blossoms

All at once the air is full
of honey bees
and the sweet stinging
of Nature

It is a short radiant season
withering unsapped
into the bee-less dark

Unlike say the buckthorn
if you touch these roots gently
there   between the boulders
you will feel the seedling stir
again   softly

Sweeping

The snow was expected.
We were not prepared
for the blizzard.

The trees like stiff brooms
quivered
against grey clouds,
compulsively tidying
the sky.

Like trees we stood
out in the swirling
snow

sweeping

sweeping.

Trees

1. White Pine, Douglas Fir, Yellow Cedar

Canadian White Pine Sawmill, Vancouver, Fraser River, 1970

They weigh heavily against our hooks and chains,
these avuncular, waterlogged Gandhians,
skulking in the sloshing flotsam.
The union steward is telling me,
in his stalwart Anglo-Dutch,
I should read Kropotkin.
He is thinking about workers,
better pay, guys at the pub, a TV.
I am considering ecology,
mutual aid, trees, co-evolution,
how far from this mephitic fog
the creaking silence,
the prickly blue-green shrug
of a windblown branch,
the soft-headed moss.
Behind us, bark dishevelled,
the old tatterdemalions
scream with the band saws,
karaoke blues from hell.

They are just trees,
after all, I tell myself. This is not family.
At the green chain, my shoulders ache
from yanking them, resisting,
away from the glare and clattering steel
onto the cool stacks
in the dark behind me.

2. Maple, Aspen, Fir

South Cape Chin, Niagara Escarpment, 2000

The wooden furniture creaks,
falls silent.
Does it accuse?
A table. A pencil. A roof over my head. A door.
Out there, arthritic roots cling
to rocks along the escarpment,
clawing up the precipice,
leaning out, giddily,
into the spray, gathering in hollows
along the crest. Roots unclenched,
they topple across my path.
My body returns, again and again
to that quiet breathing,
the lifegiving *sotto voce* sigh,
the light patter of sun and rain
drizzling from the canopy.
I cannot get enough of walking
among the trees,
their thoughtless, perfect love
that holds,
and lets me go.

3. The craft

Oh sacred grove, now wounded,
what can requite thy worth?

Word, grooved with caring hand to word,
a craft to bear us, earth to earth.

Endangered Species

1. The Disappearance

When your friends leave
you are a shrub

and they are a snake
whose head thinks itself
already across the path
but whose body remains
entangled in you

They are a cat who clings
pulled away from you
so you are torn
by the persistence of its love

They are crows
who leave in the Fall not knowing
they will return

2. The Sighting

I sit in a boat
on an unruffled lake
mist paling in the muffled dawn
The water breaks   sploosh
just at the edge of my vision

I look to see a spray
of silver flowers trailing
silver rippling necklace rings
encircling
an empty centre

I am not sure
what I have seen
I can only report
I am not sure
what I am remembering
what might have been

Two loons drift by
into the lifting mist
three little ones
paddling madly after

For what we are about to receive

A dead snake
A dead mouse
A dead beaver
A hustle of ants
A dervish of flies
A whisperation of maggots
A propagation of fungi
A bedlam of bacteria
A solemnity of soil
A daisy
A sweet pea
An Indian paintbrush
A prettiness of poison ivy

A man declaiming
at the cliff's edge,
"One Day All This,"
with a waving of arms,
and slow-circle-dancing
beneath the diamond
sky, slips on a merry fop
of moss.

His footing lost,
he tumbles ignominiously
to a heap of rocks below.

The lichens
puff a grateful grace.

Fauna

A Man Sits Naked

A man sits naked
on a mountain
in the fog.
He feels the cool breath
of nature on his skin, the clean
press of rock against his bum.
He feels solidarity
with his species, at one
with all living things
back into the ancient mists before time,
back to slimy things climbing
through algae and equisetum
up the shore to earth, stones, roots.
He comes down
with stress-induced pulmonary infection.
He learns about the laws of Nature.

A man sits naked
on a street corner
in the sunlight.
He feels a crowd of eager eyes
scanning his body.
He feels the palms of the law
on his buttocks.
He is taken down
for questioning, fined for mischief,
put behind bars. He feels solidarity
with immigrants the world over,
at one with barefoot peasants
displaced from their lands, herded
among bent palms, through fevered marshes
to the edge of the menacing sea.
He learns about the laws of Culture.

A man puts on his clothes.
They let him out of jail.
He climbs a mountain.
He sits on a rock
in bright cold morning light.
He remembers a man
stepping from a boat into the surf,
waves sucking at his cuffs.
He recalls a fragile newborn baby,
held in his chapped hands.
He hears the gulls,
scudding down the wind-waves

crying, crying, crying.

Faith for the Long Trek Out of Olduvai

I meant what I said, and I said what I meant—
an elephant's faithful one hundred percent.—Dr. Seuss

Fill your mind with elephants,
long trunks uncurling upward
in the sun, into a rustling crinoline of leaves.
Fill your mind with trees, tall trunks swaying.
Fill your mind with hippopotami
smooth and yawning, bum-skinned,
funny, in the river.
Fill your mind with villages and children
running past with sticks and cast-off wheels.
Fill your pride with lions
and secretary birds
and a bouncing family of warthogs
trotting past.
Fill your office with secretary birds
scripting long-tailed letters on blue
stationery.
Fill your dreams with shade
from the Serengeti sun
and cheetahs, quiet, resting.
Fill your life with larks at the feeder,
with your pet dog
and the cat in your lap.
Fill your town with good people
driving in good cars
down good roads.
Fill your morning with a good run
in fresh country air; imagine yourself
as a gazelle, spritely sailing over endless grass.

Fill your head with dreams.

Fill your reveries with deserts
and sacks of charcoal beside the road.
Fill your sack with elephant bones
and contraband ivory.
Fill your village with galumphing hippopotami
exploding through maize and nightmares,
flocks of chickens, screaming children, clay walls
fluorescing in the starry night.
Fill your Serengeti with lions fighting over
the remains of your Lhasa Apso,
with your pet cat having a lark,
for dinner, in the meadow,
with a vulture just above, pausing for grace,
a stationary moment in the sky,
then dropping in for dinner.
Fill your mind with air conditioning
and smog advisories.
Fill your office with overworked secretaries
and your cafeteria with a bouncing family of warthogs.
Fill your dreams with cheetahs,
sprinting, warm-breathed, just behind
you. Prey.

Pray for emptiness.
Pray for rain. Pray for shade.

And when there's nothing left,
keep walking.

Something is Missing

It Cannot Be Caught

Our bodies are
the interslipping of a thousand fish
fins sensing almost touch
a thousand neural tips
in playful synchronicity   all rhyme
for no earthy reason

It calls for a poem
It begs for a net
When I oblige
what do I get? Haddock flopping
in a slippery pile
and   between the lines   into the deep
lost blue   a silver flutter

Friday the poet eats fish
sticks with ketchup   a good meal
but something short
of a religious experience

Breaking Free the Whales

On Loving Earth Not Wisely, But Too Well

In a kind of wild exuberance

caught perhaps from the wet lash
of arctic wind
or the icy slap of brine
against our thighs
or the glimpse of bright sun glinting
from their hulls, we threw ourselves
into the thick of it,
the thick ice crust
creaking, bending under
the sheer weight of our dancing.

No rewards could supplant
our surge into the swell of open sea,
no cracks in our seeming solid prow,
no listing to starboard,
no regrets. Even knowing we've polluted
good intentions with these giant fantasies,
confusing poor navigational genes
with nature's pure desires,
nothing can overpower

this sense: the dry-lipped tropic heat
of too much loving
however ill-conceived,

this sight: their gentle laugh
like a spout like a flag unfurled,

like a hand waving
as they crest a distant wave,

while under us
the ice crackles.

Milton Hikes the Bruce Trail

Cape Chin, Ontario

And that last morning
in the brilliant sun,
let a thousand trembling
aspen leaves descend in ruffling waves
of flippant silvery-green fans,
to bury me, tittering,
"Have you seen it yet? Isn't it wonderful?"
while all around, the cedars
stand, solemn, and serenely warm.

And on my deathbed,
to the *Lepus americanus*
boosted up on floppy snowshoe hare
hand-me-down shoes,
nibbling a high black cherry bush leaf
and of a sudden with those big brown eyes
round with constant amazement,
catching a glimpse of a naked man
eating a bagel,
let me announce, arms wide,
on my last legs, that I have never felt for anything
such all-embracing love.
As life slips me away, I want to see his worried nose,
his up-kicked heels, the high-tailing of it all.

Did you ever startle a rattlesnake on the trail?
Did you talk to him there, all curled up on the wrinkled rock,
the devil himself, his tail poised next to his head,
a cute, quivering, coquettish gesture?
Did he tremble his mother-of-pearl castanets?
Did he cast a spell to keep you
from the only place on the trail

where the sun was
just right? Did you wonder
about Satan and the light?
I hedged past among the junipers,
with their little berries, their sad eyes
with too much powder blue eyeshadow,
and their pouty blue painted-on mouths,
and when I squished them between my fingers,
the bitter scent spoke of an empire's sad tonic,
the djinn of a tropic afternoon.

Later, when I peed beside the path,
seeking similarities
between the snake's sleek, muscled coils
and my pizzle, I remembered how his cocoa-coloured
hexagonal scales made maps of Africa and Borneo,
and I wondered at an empire of belonging lost,
And I remembered how, in the Fall,
before the cold white death comes stalking,
the leaves turn shiny reds and yellows,
mottled with chocolate, or liver spots.
I checked my foreskin
for a colour change.
I wish now I'd gone back
to talk it over with the snake
just brother to brother, guy talk,
one last time, how our minds conquered,
how we lost the earth.

Let me one final time be watched
by *Tamias striatus* as I sip
a glass of peppery Shiraz,
something to give a little pizzazz to my afternoon
fig newton, and watch the lake turn darker shades of blue
and silver. Let her rise up to see

what I am eating. Let me say, Hi, Tammy.
Let her eyes be calm and her whiskers uncertain.
Let her nibble suddenly under her arm,
then dash into the quiet cedars.
Let me think about how blessed I have been.
Let me in that final breath cast from
my fact-bound brain, the litany of rodent fleas,
of hantavirus pulmonary syndrome, of plague.

Before I can pronounce some pithy epitaph,
distract me with a wash of wind
rushing and splashing
high in the maples and trembling aspen,
like the waves on the lakeshore,
kissing the shore pebbles, pulling back,
sighing just a little, then, leaning over too far,
falling, and kissing and kissing again.

And then, that one last time,
I too shall kiss the pebbles on the shore.

Teilhard de Chardin Surfs the Internet

We speak with voices
neither of men nor angels.
We speak with the ephemeral complexity
of electrons, a conversation
of sand castles, articulating perplexity,
retreating to a sigh of candy wrappers, pop cans,
foam and kelp-litter, scraps of garbage
information, dissimulation,
thoughts for gulls to squabble over.
And as the sea sucks back,
a crab, incredible, unthinking, hard
quotidian experience, a wonder of survival,
scuttles over the traces
of our castles. All over the world,
on the beaches of the internet,
you can hear the hissing intake of breath.
All of evolution's come to this
anticipation, this wondrous
rising wave. For just one cresting second,
in tightening bellies, tumbling over
flashing sand, stars, water, air,
and just before
the flotsam engulfs us,
we shall have spoken everything,
understood
nothing,
the sea will sigh,
and, rising sluggishly, heave:
just one more try.

On Occasion

A Poem for Giorgio

This is the street you walk along
after a rain, the concrete glistening
under the greenish glare of streetlights.
The lights are going out.
People are settling down.
The world is blowing up.

The flies this year are irrepressible.
They buzz in my coffee cup,
copulate on the rice, rest on my earlobe.
They are planning what colour the drapes will be
after the war.

I am almost 40, when life, I am told, begins.
To celebrate my birthday, a friend gave me a blow-up
of a colonoscopy picture, and I realize,
that there is a light at the end of the tunnel,
but we are at the wrong end,
looking into the darkness.

I turn, and see a street from 1967,
a clearing in the jungle
an overgrown path between fear, inadequacy, and,
breaking through the low-slung clouds,
an unexpected blaze of sun.

This street I am on, Giorgio,
I have started running down,
my habits flapping behind me,
the fumes flowering in my nose.
I have clearance from the tower.
I am almost out of breath.
My feet rotate like wheels, like feet in a cartoon.
We can fly, Giorgio. It's all in arms control.

Arms away!

I am lifting off.
My eyes are on the light.
Giorgio, flying deeper into the twentieth century,
are you there?

The Poetry of Work

1. Retrospective

Ten years later
it is possible
to write poetry
about the worst of jobs
Of that job in the sawmill
only the scenery remains
waxed cold two-by-fours
clamming on my palms
the roughness and perfume of cedar
old calf leather aprons
smoke signals from a plastic thermos cup
And I can't recall how the jackhammer
vandalized my eardrums
that summer I worked concrete
I remember sleeping well at night
When I belaboured layouts
for a small religious publisher
I was so tight with angry prophecies
all gone now   It snowed heavily that year
our first of marriage
We were a beast of fur and flesh
snortling
in disturbed hibernation

2. Contemporary

The cow I am examining
is a created beast
dependent on others
for her livelihood
She is a milk production quota
that never quite meets itself
She is a metaphor
for the farmer
who is dependent on a multi-
national corporation
The farmer is symbolic of all men
and the corporation
is a Calvinistic god
that is a metaphor
for a graven image
Even that illusion fails
The dark barn I stand in
has no running water and no electricity
I have my hand in the cow's rectum
In another ten years
I may find this poetic

Roots

not about Rudy Wiebe, but for him

Rudy Wiebe, wiping the sweat from his brow,
calls a spade a spade.
He has a spade in his hands.
He is digging a hole near Winnipeg
in the middle of a potato field.
He has blisters on his hands.
He has roots on the brain.
He is looking for his roots.
One foot down he unearths
a nest of potatoes.
Two feet later he has an aching soul
and a sore foot.

His spade has struck a bone.
It is a dry bone.
It gets up and walks around.
Rudy is not sure if it is an ankle bone
or a hip bone.
It may be the bone of a buffalo
dropped by an Indian's arrow or of an Indian
killed by Mennonite good fortune.
Perhaps a Mennonite died here
of overwork and too many potatoes.
Most likely it is the bone of a cow
that choked on a potato.
Rudy Wiebe cannot tell for sure
what kind of bone it is.
He watches the bone walk out to the road
and head toward town.
The people in Winnipeg ignore the bone.
To them, it is just another drunk Indian.

After the bone
Rudy Wiebe takes a lunch break.
He sits beside the hole and eats
rollkuchen with watermelon.
After lunch he continues his search.
There is a lot of dirt in the hole.
There is a lot of dirt in Winnipeg.
The bone gets tired of Winnipeg
and comes back out to the field.
It sits on the nest of potatoes
and watches the top of Rudy's head
going up and down in the hole
between sprays of dirt.

By nightfall Rudy Wiebe
is up to his ears in dirt
but he still hasn't found any roots.
He tilts back his hard hat
shoulders the spade
and trudges home,
bone in hand.
How was your day? asks his mother.
No luck, he says
hanging up his hat.
Maybe you are right.
Maybe my roots are in Russia.

My my, says his mother.
You have enough dirt behind your ears
to grow potatoes.
Rudy pulls a nest of potatoes
out from behind his ear.
Rudy and his widowed mother are very poor.
For supper they have potato soup

with a bone in it.
When I was a girl in Russia,
says Rudy's mother,
we ate this all the time.

Emmanuel

thousands of fathers dead before are no comfort
in the presence of my dead father

promises of golden mansions   deformed angels
bubble gum and trumpets are no consolation

these religious politicians who speak of sleep
to their adoring lambs they do not know
my God   my dark forsaken God

the only comfort after volcanic ruptures
skies split by lightning and the thunderous
toppling of heaven's gilded pillars is this

dead silence of wood and wet rock
and the solitary punctuation of a frog
like a comma   promising

The Door

My father worked with horses
as a boy
tugging the great sweating rumps
along a straight furrow

Later he worked in the church
though I would be unkind
to draw the obvious parallel

He turned just as he left
the sun in his eyes
so that he had to shade them
with his hand
He waved and smiled
I could see the black-maned horses
glistening with sweat
streaked with dust
The field was not quite done

He was gone

The body suddenly ungiving
the sun extinguished
a field cast
into chill darkness

It is not sleep
no slick and golden road
to glory   The body's carriage
shockless and numb
left shattered by the way
death is death is death

the slow walk to what is
I AM

All words are vanity
revolutions benedictions bombs three cheers for
these repetitions
all in vain
In the end the door opens
Someone is there   a guide perhaps

On the Death of a Father

When the shadow passes,
you quiver like a small,
hairless mouse, and freeze.
The talons sting
more deeply in the heart
than you expected.
The breathless flight
so far above the happy
trees, house, friends
you barely recognize,
seems forever.

You are left
alone
at the bottom of the sky,
at your doorstep.
At the foot of the stairs
you see him, turning.
He smiles.

When you return
to the kitchen there are someone's children,
a strange, tall man,
cereal in a dish, the telephone
ringing. You cannot remember
what you were doing
before the news. You
run into the street,
looking for signs of familiarity.
When the postman arrives
you hug him, fiercely,
until he pushes you away.

There are no letters.
There is no word.
A phrase turns over and over
in the unutterable darkness
within you.
You search the sky for a shadow
of meaning. You search the faces
of the family standing in your door;
they are waiting, even the cat
between their legs, for a sign.

This sentence is for life.
It will end with a question mark,
or an exclamation;
this cannot be predicted
from the subject or the verb,
from your vague smile,
the giddy rising of your heart from the depths,
or the knife-sharp bends as part of you comes
out of solution.

There is no pause.
You are already in the kitchen
peeling carrots
for lunch.

My Mother's Heart Attack

Just a touch of the flu,
she told her sister,
sucking back the pain and nausea.
She carried her bags to the plane.
I should home be going
to get some rest,
she said, dabbing the perspiration
from her brow.

When my mother had a heart attack
the sidewalk dropped away behind me,
a huge, creeping crater,
deeper than the Manitoba gravel pits
where teenagers disappeared without a trace
into the blue water.
I had to keep walking, then,
straining not to run,
knowing the cement was crumbling
after me.

The pit can smell your fear.
If you consider fleeing
it will make a sudden, leaping bite
and pull you down.
Like a Blue Heeler,
it is just moving you along.
It knows where you must go.

My mother has seen it all,
from the Czar to Stalin,
Manning and Vander Zalm—
It's all the same.
Your husband dies.

Your children grow up.
Floods and famines,
politicians, families,
accountants, visionaries:
there is nothing new under the sun.

I just keep walking.
I am starting to hear voices,
from the pit, maybe,
or just in my head.
I do not recognize them.
I fear they might be
Haida, Ainu, a Tibetan minority
forgotten even by the Tibetans, an inchoate chorus
of impending extinctions,
clamouring for a mouth.

All I can think of is my mother,
her silence, my tongue.
Under a supple, radiant, red-gold maple tree,
I stop, transfixed,
my heart ringing into my ears.
I ignore the wet nose sniffing
at my heel,
puzzled at how, under the operatic flare
of this mad October sun,
the twisted syntax
of my mother tongue
now from my lips is falling.

The Gift

for Mother, who has survived revolution, civil war, drought, famine, being orphaned, emigration, servant work, motherhood, widowhood, and much more, on her 75th birthday

After the first sharp cry
it is not a question, this life,
of what has been survived.
It is what has survived.

It is not your father gone,
swarthy faces at the window with guns.
In the kitchen, it is Mother's hum,
a cup of fresh warm milk, and a bun.

It is not Mother reduced to the bone's
terrible whisper, nor a house abandoned.
It is the train like a bright snake amid the ruins,
a bird soaring, crying, in its flight home.

It is not the hopelessness of loss,
rude officials at greasy shipyards, and dust.
It is a young woman from overseas, the kindness in her face,
setting out the doctor's tea in blue china cups.

Of that new land as flat as plautdietsch
where even the zwieback loomed significant,
and pluma moos for all the Englisch knew
was some kind of deer to shoot

and a horse a husband five bushy-haired
kids a house—several houses, one finally with no steep stairs—a real freez-
er for meat buns and cookies and a recreation room
to hide the television, we can really only claim

the cookies, which we did, still frozen,
as our first tangible recollection.
But even this—our remembering and remembering of remembrance—
will pass, and our children's.

It is not the quartz-sharp grit deeply clasped
by the heart which we inherit, nor the pain's lingering grasp.
It is you, here, now, the rich, opaquely buffed layers
of your life, like a pearl before us.

The Next Ten Years

Let us be messy lovers,
drunk before breakfast,
spilling the white milk everywhere.
Let our love be a stain
on the world's tablecloth.

Our love is beans.
O love we have spilled them.
They have grown feet.
They are running to the children
running to the neighbours
running to El Salvador
Somalia and Poland.
They are nosing underground.

They shall come up wantonly,
tipsily green, leaning
arms entangled in the wind,
clutching a spray of white flowers.

Natural Love

There is no love in clouds,
for though I cycle with the best morale
they time their heed to nature's call
just when I take the road.

There is no love in soil,
the righteous sweat I pour into the compost hole
upheaved, discarded by raccoons
who from my spare cuisine recoil.

There is no love in air,
for though I use no aerosol
winter abuses with an icy claw,
and summer spites me with an ozone stare.

There is no love in cats;
although I feed them low-ash friendly
crunch, and fondle them, they bring me fleas,
and flopping birds, though, thankfully, not rats.

And even the tomatoes, fed
and watered with a loving hand, respond
with bugs and fungus and
at harvest time, with being soft, and dead.

Oh love, come read me now,
for nowhere is love writ but where your tongue
inscribes, and nowhere read but where your lingering
fingers tread the braille, and all that nature knows

is scripted by the tussle
of our bodies' calligraphic brush.

The Time of Our Lives

I am having the time of my life
digging up an old pine stump
with my daughter
in the bright Fall sunshine.
Everything I need to know about life
and death is in this moment.

The spade is singing
among the white-collared mushrooms:
Praise to the Fungi Imperfecti,
the Fusaria and the Cladospores.
The hatchet chops a tune
into the wood's soft heart:
Praise to the wood lice, the earthworms,
millipedes, hister beetles, common black
ground beetles, the slugs like ushers
waving their antennae at the calamitous lightspill.
Please close the door. The show's in progress.
Praise to the unseen saints of Gaia,
the Bacilli, the Clostridia,
and the pearly Micrococci.

Praise to the myriad of unseen
crawlies, the forgotten ones,
the bond breakers, hewers of cellulose
who make possible this uprooting.

After so many years
a friend becomes part of you.
Where the roots begin and the earth ends,
where pleasure, where pain,
where wishful memory, or truth,
cannot be dissected.

No point in spading here.
It is I myself who would be uprooted
if I uprooted you.

Time is an arrow
only in the briefest bug-life fragments,
and at the meteoric limits of our growth.
Where we live time is an inchworm,
rhythms of seasons and spades,
roots broken and re-sprung.
The stump is lifting
under the pry of my spade.
A mouth opens below,
a dark mouth singing
soft fleshy things,
singing multi-footed messengers,

singing a lieder of cycles
the carbon cycle, the nitrogen cycle,
the water, the sulfur,
singing of the microscopic fixers,
singing lustily, with full synthesizer backup,
in chlorophyllic warbles,

who make me, Hominus Imperfecti,
possible, and you, and our sons
and our daughters and
brightly, in the blue, sharp sunshine,
as the roots lift free, I am dug in,
rooted,
earthworms, beetles, fungi,
bacilli all around me,
skittling up the spade handle toward me, singing:

Welcome home.
Your turn is next.

Man about the House

Homestead

I built this place,
searched out the strong
green words,
chopped and trimmed them,
chinked them with commas,
thatched a title
between the frozen page
and hardwood frame.

I have been waiting for you
here, beside the fire,
between the lines,
cords of unused words
stacked up all around me.
I've left enough unsaid
to keep us warm

all winter.

A Bill from the Power Company

It begins in New Guinea
with veneration of our ancestors.
It begins with love of wisdom and intelligence.
It begins with admiring the dead.
It begins with our cleverness
and our envy.
It begins with eating the brains
of those whom we admire,
with women and children first.
It ends with Kuru, a spongy Jacuzzi
of laid back prions, engulfing the brain.
It ends with a young woman
throwing herself into the fire.

It begins in America with a dust bowl,
with the world war's devastation.
It begins with hungry children
in Europe and Africa.
It begins with our cleverness
and our lust for power and our tractors.
It begins with cows coming in from the green
wilderness in droves.
It begins with praise of hamburgers
on every tongue.
It begins with some spare change
after shopping for food,
and the thrill of a new car.
It begins with recycling, with efficiency,
with cow-eat-cow.
It ends with old men
hungry for power.
It ends with a mob of mad cows
fed to power stations,
shimmering up in smoke

from the incinerators.

It begins with love of life.
It begins in a white coat.
It begins with cutting and sewing.
It begins with new drugs.
It begins with our cleverness
and our fear of death.
It begins with ingesting those
who have what we want.
It begins with blood transfusions,
with hearts, kidneys, and corneal transplants,
with bone marrow and dura mater.
It ends with rabies, with AIDs,
with a slow toppling of prions
across the brain.
It ends with a young man,
unable to walk, unable to speak
his own name.

It begins with flowers and wine.
It begins with clever conversation.
It begins with the love of children,
of making them, and, surprisingly, caring for them.
It begins with a house and a car
and a school and a computer.
It ends with paying
the power bill.
It comes round
to huddling by a campfire
playing old guitars,
singing plaintive melodies,
and, in the ash-black darkness at our backs,
the sound of cows or bears foraging,
and the slow sigh of a rising moon.

Bird Of Prey

Turning high above the clefts and hillocks
in the clear silence
in the cool silken blue sweep of sky,
a sharp, anxious fear comes piercing like a sudden cry:
is it my turn to be home feeding the nestlings?
have I left the oven on?
does some hunter have her sights on me?
is this merely my stupid fear of heights?
am I a white male?
was my first language German?
is this all my fault?
when I arrive home, will the nest be empty?

The land shimmers and lifts.
A small brown mouse quivers in a furry cleft.
The thoughtless plunge engulfs me,
down through darkness
the bright bottomless thrill
the wriggling flash of life, the quick throb
here in my talons
gotcha!

The wild furry thing is mine.
I squeeze and squeeze
until my fears are still
until the thing is still

and I am lifting, giddy, full of light.
The clefts and hillocks fall away from me
so far away. I am again the cool dark point,
the heavens turning slowly at my wingtips.
From my claw-tip drops the frail, wet-feathered nestling.

The arrow spears again, cupid's shadow
the hunter with her finger on the bow
of my regrets for what I've done, have not done,
have undone, cannot remember,
have not conceived.
The perfect two-kid two-car TV CD green lawn predator
I once despised
I have become.
I have no right to be here.
This is no one's sky.

There is no place to be
but here.
This is the story of my life.

The True Meaning of Being a Man

I am peeling an onion for the borscht.
It is firm as a bulging bicep.
I split the grainy, weather-beaten outer skin.
It peels off cleanly, unequivocally.
Inside: the absolute onion, colour of old ivory,
smooth and sure as a man's career.
Curious, I make another incision—
another layer bares itself, whiter and more vulnerable
than the last. I cut again, and again
two more shells open, delicate and lopsided
as a lover's balls.
The odour of this flesh, pungent as acid,
incisive as a prophet's warning,
stings my nostrils,
brings tears to my eyes.
I become obsessed, attacking
carving my relentless way
through flesh and bone and brain
with the razor-edged calculus of a knife,
each layer paler, more translucent
more precious and righteous than the last.
Ruthlessly I chop them up,
cast them into boiling broth.
Finally, eyes gleaming,
drenched in manful sweat,
I have it: the tiniest of pearls,
unmitigated onion, essence of cognizance,
gallstone of intellect.
Religiously, I lower the triumphant blade.
My hands are trembling.

"Aren't you putting a lot of onions in the borscht?"
my wife asks.

The Ecology of Poetry

If tomorrow is at the door
and today, dishevelled on the couch,
still hasn't had her coffee,
don't let him in. Tomorrow can ruin today.
He'll drag out the better part of your day,
the pink skirt maybe,
and worry ragged holes into it
like a nesting hamster.
Do you need that?

Yesterday is bad enough,
and last week sprawled on the guest bed
and a few years ago scattered
about like floor cushions. Party guests
who stayed the night, they have bad breath and hangovers.
Like leftovers, plates of them, rotting around me.

We should all have compost heaps
spaded deep into our souls,
with modest wooden covers. Honey,
could you empty the can under the sink?
It's smelling ripe already—
bits of pain, scraps of ecstasy,
moments full of people, love, regret,
wine and maudlin verse.

The days of throwing out are over.
The world's already littered with our junk—
personal anger, revenge, passions made over
into public illusions of righteousness:
submarines named Corpus Christie and all those phallic
missiles. But if you just keep them in
you'll rot along with them, a confused heap
of smelly memories. The neighbours will complain.

The compost heap is singing.
If I don't sing along it will drive me insane.
If I sing, the neighbours will know I already am.
So I already am. I cannot help myself,
singing. I am eating my own leftovers,
ludicrously, tragically, as if I enjoy them.
I do enjoy them.

That is why I am here, near midnight,
kneading this lump of doughy past.
Tomorrow morning, fresh biscuits.
Oblivious to the future's wry shadow
slipping in, a cold gust tailing
the complaining cat, I'll go out.
All the way to the office, whistling.

All the old familiar notes.
A whole new song.

Peaceful Linguistics

Peace is a word to be coupled with
time   at the end
at the end of a busy
a busy and repetitive workday
I long for a little
a little time for
a little
and quiet
peace a word to be couched
with nick as in the saint
as in a person whose conscience was nicked
in the shave of
time   a small word to be put with
out   a breather a moment to think
before the final play
for peace   a game to be wrestled
with talks which start are called off and
swing on with the mood of a popular tic
which returns us to time and to
peace   a word to be married with full
and the fulness
of time
which is our end

Sunday Morning

Crow stands beside the highway,
a priest in black satin
casting his censorious beak
this way and that
under a heavenly crown
of radiant autumn trees.

It is only a matter of time
before a feast, served on God's silver
splatter, comes to his cocky lordship:
a fat squirrel, a tail-wagging dog,
maybe a toddler in overalls,
an old woman with a shawl,
a man escaping voices in a car.

I pass Crow on my way to church.
We shall sing in four parts, full force,
at the tops of our lungs,
voices from the past breaching,
at long last, these damned bodies,
carrying our souls with them,
releasing them
in a furious tide of glory.

But this morning, the pianist has a mind of her own.
She wants to transform us
into instruments for her glory.
Her fingers thrum over the ivory ribs,
creating her own bone-rattling
disharmonies, voices to haunt
this patriarchal wilderness we share.
Just when our singing is about to peak,
she leaves us dangling
from a trembling clef.

She knows that all the bad things
in her life were because
she was a woman
and all the bad things
that happened to me
were well-deserved.
She knows, knowing myself,
I will concur.

The woman at the pulpit,
black hair spread back
like raven's wings
fixes her eyes on me.
She speaks of bodies and boundaries,
the body of Christ,
the consummating heat of God.
She has me on my back over the lectern.
Rising white, glistening, luminous and erect
above me, her penetrating insights
reduce me to moans and quivers.

And I am lifted up
into a brave new heaven,
above, finally,
all that history, all those cocky victories
returning now to haunt me,
all those souls rescued from their bodies,
all those rescued bodies, to save our souls,
the children saved at birth,
saved from their better selves,
saved into this war zone, this songless desert,
these chronic poetry shortages,
lineups for a scrap of humour,
and the long silent night
surrounding us:

this is how the world ends.

This is how the world should end:
a small act of kindness
at the moment I close my eyes,
consumed among the cords of flaming
Wesleyan choruses,

a gentle hand somewhere on my body
a cool, indifferent sun glancing through the car window,
Crow in the rear-view mirror
anxiously waiting by the empty highway.

Conversion Experience

The Powers were everywhere
the still small voice stilled
Leaves I heard or fresh cold snow
or steam perhaps escaping
My heart was tamed my brain professioned
the untrustworthy rhythms of my blood re-schooled
the black tunnels of my id mined
I was being packaged for export
I was being run in the national interest
I was only following orders

Sneaking down the back alleys of my gut
ready for my soul's ignominious exit
in a cloud of gas there in the foulest dungeon
I almost tripped over Him
My God what are you doing here?
Coward! He answered *Fool! Traitor! Get back*
there!

Stung as in a prairie blizzard
I reeled back through whimpering
bloodswamps up clambering
the cold rocks of power
into the trees no forest
can be seen for
The government was caught off guard
by the pure rage of my love
Was this a brief? a speech?
Had I come before the wrong committees?
They wanted my credentials
Was I a royal commission? They couldn't
find the right papers They wanted
to be out of opposition They wanted

to be in luck   They wanted
to deal with the issues   They wanted
to see my social insurance number

I do not remember it all
my tongue a whip   the tables overturned
Not alone I was   we were
in the streets again   doctors
cooks diaper washers computer scientists
poets farmers God help us even veterinarians
all of us singing arresting traffic
without a warrant   unscrewing
the missiles at our backs   unhinging
the industry of death
singing around a great fire
enough to make even the most tempered
of steel hearts soften   singing
without children in our arms   wondering
at our lack of professional decor   wondering
at the money we were losing   not being
at work   wondering at the beauty
of it all

Later   I was
a child alone
in the wrecked aged   chambers of my heart
papers swirling in the wind
the hiss somewhere of steam escaping
the voice of God   perhaps
And outside
or somewhere in a guarded classroom
in my brain   the Powers re-grouping
voices of children playing Star Wars

Generations

Matthew tells me
that every day another species
disappears.
When mother sea turtles clamber up the beach
people cut pieces
right out of the shell
for jewellery.
Baleen whales are killed
for no apparent reason.

Tonight at bedtime he says, Dad
you know how Nature
is always changing?
Well I want something different
for next Christmas,
a real Transformer.
What you bought me this year
was a Decepticon.

Decepticons are the bad guys,
he says, knowing that to me
they look the same. Transformers, he adds, are good.
At seven years he is telling me parables,
sees through my layers of masks,
my masquerades of change.

Of course I am imagining this precocity,
yet where else do our children dwell
but in the heavens/hells we think for them?
This is the essence, is it not, of minding children?

I feel myself coming loose,
another parental sacrifice

to the cosmic tooth fairy,
like Matthew's tooth, bleeding at the gums
where Melissa bumped him at recess.

For a brief period
his tongue will speak into the gap,
and then a new, sharp, tooth will push up
into a world I cannot imagine.

What to Pray For

Rebecca lying in bed
stares blue-eyed into the space
just below the stippled ceiling
where God must surely be
kicks up her pink pyjama-clad legs
and prays Please God let no one
in the whole world
be sick or lonely

That's impossible, says Matthew
when she's done She balks
at his realism rolls over
and goes to sleep in protest

The next night legs tucked modestly
under the covers she prays Please God
let no one in the whole world get sick
most of the time
and let Oma and John Rempel
not be lonely

The Snow Fort

Once a year we built a fort—
Matthew, Rebecca, and I—
from hardened snow, till our cheeks hurt
from the bite of the wintry blue sky.

Once a year we stacked the chunks
of uneven, prickly ice
till, walls over eyeballs, out of the wind,
we vanished without a trace.

Only our bodies, once a year
kept up the appearance of us,
while we clambered misty snowbound peaks
and hummed Amazing Grace.

We only came back if the sky fell down
and bonked us on the head
or someone was calling Dinner Time!
or our toes felt like cold lead.

Yes, once a year we built that place—
Matthew, Rebecca, and I—
cheek by toe, on fire, in ice,
biting back at the wintry blue sky.

You are Not a Cat

a father's advice to his children

Make friends. Challenge them. Wait for them.
Let your friends go. Make new ones. Welcome the old ones
back. Stand by them. Sit by them.
Worry with them. Think of something bigger
of which you are a part. Create a community. Enlarge it.
Make a place for wasps, walnut trees and grackles.
Include Germany, Jordan, Belize, Indonesia
and Davis Inlet. Listen to everything
around you.

Grow up. Laugh about it. Love your innocence.
Nurture it. Love your experience. Be complicated.
Live simply. Play. Be amazed. Doubt.
When in doubt, trust.
When trust is betrayed, doubt
and trust again.
Be disillusioned.

If you are a cat, be a cat.
If you are an ant, be an ant.
If you got through grade one, get real:
you are neither cat nor insect.
Dig a compost hole.
Sit with the cat, watching ants and squirrels.
Water the roses.
Listen for worms with the robins.

Have strong opinions. Argue.
Change your mind.
Make enemies. Love your enemies.
Fight for their rights. Demand your responsibilities.
Relax. Let go.

Never forget. Always forgive.
If you can't remember, let it go:
if it needs you, it will
come back.

Let the buck stop with you.
If you have a buck, share it.
Read books.
Talk to your father. Listen
to your mother. Feel
the wind on your face. Feel
the waters around you. Rise up.
Pray without ceasing.

When your cat dies,
cry your heart out.
Return your heart to its proper place.
Do an autopsy to see why
the cat died.
Remember this for your next cat.
Bury her in the back yard.
Plant a rose bush over her.
Prune the bush.
Pile cow manure around it.
Relish the scent.
Cultivate your powers of observation.
Look again.

Lose a good argument.
Be devastated.
Do good. Do it well.
Succeed. Fail. Grow.

Use e-mail. Write. Call.
Keep secrets. Share them over tea
with muffins. Be a character
in many others' lives.
Think in stories. Talk in parables.
Hum to yourself.
Sing with your friends.

Drop by for no reason.
If we are not in,
drop a note in the mailbox.

Just say hi.

Tante Tina Talks

Tante Tina Talks About Her Man

He was a schlingel, my man Doft,
since long already
before I had him,
but this he later forgot.
We came once over to dinner
at their house at the Namaka farm
all aufgedressed from church,
close around the table,
the steak in sauce so good
from in the oven all through church baking
you could eat it with a spoon,
and potatoes mashed with a loch
in the middle for gravy.
We were all smelling so much
we could hardly hold ourselves for eating
and Mr. Reimer he little Doft asks to pray
with his brother Pete.
We are all thinking they will say
"Segne Vater diese Speise
Uns zur Kraft and Dir zum Preise Amen"
but together they sing
"Eetle ottle black bottle
Eetle ottle out Amen"
and then burst out laughing like horses
blowing through the nose.
Mr. Reimer was so angry
he said nothing
but the boys dragged by the neck
out to the barn
so we the cries couldn't hear.
And even after Mrs. Reimer prayed
Elsie and I were still ashamed
for being children and thinking the boys

did it for us, to show off, ja,
so we into our plates looked
and haven't much eaten.

But Doft he was never one for learning.
There was the time an Englische preacher
from the city came and spoke
about tithes and offerings
for the konferenz, and Doft has his tie
into the collection plate put. And already
once he in Bible School was
Bob Friesen from Winnipeg came to visit
to the farm and Doft let him ride
the one horse who loved the barn
more than anything
so when they went out it was slow
like going to the front to get saved
but coming back
it was fast like a pig running
and when they through the door of the barn
back galloped his knees
scraping clean the skin off,
the Friesen boy his pants filled
and Doft was in the straw laughing.

We have ourselves found
in Bible School and have been married
when the dust storms were thick in the air
and the wind like a choir of chicken manure
from the coulee was singing.
My white dress and Doft's navy suit and our faces
all were grey
so in the pictures
we already old looked yet.

The more hard we worked
the more the Lord blessed
the more pious was my man
until how many were the cows
and how big was the tractor
and the word of the Lord
all were the same.

The two girls came
and could zucker platz make
but my man had no platz except for Haenschen
who came after
and then only in the barn.
Haenschen, he was just like his father
and that last time he Doft to the barn called
Come quick to see
so he through the door went
and down the milk pail on his head
is spilling—
after the wide pants and the dancing
that was the last thing.
Doft so hard hit him with the stick
until the blood came
and after Haenschen for sure
nothing of the farm wanted
and in his fancy hosen to the city went
and from church ist abgefallen.
My man is sitting then on the milk stool
and nothing saying.
Was ist zu sagen?

Then there came only work,
and no blessing.
Only once was he hitting me
when I something said

but after he just stayed
from the house.

And then came the stroke.
I had to take him to the bathroom
and from the bed uplifting
and every day the Bible reading.
Always he to the wall looked only.
He had no tongue.
Once Haenschen came back
and by the bed stood
but the two schlingels
not talking
like two old pfeffernusse
to crack your teeth on
sitting after Christmas alone
on a kitchen plate.
It is past the time for eating
and they sit there only
remembering for you
that here the family once was.

At the funeral around the open box with Doft
we have stood for the picture,
Haenschen and me and Frieda and Katie.
I am thinking
so bad it wasn't
I wouldn't it again do.

I want only once more at the piano
to be playing
and my man still with his hair
cut around like with a topf over the head
and his cheeks red from the wind
singing in tenor

"Ich weiss einen Strom, dessen herrliche Flut
fliesst wunderbar stille durchs Land."

Then my heart like a mad goose is uprising
snapping and hissing
and I have to sit down on the bench
so much hurt there is.
"Haenschen," I say, "Friedchen, Kaetchen,
there is no more comfort for me.
Ya, if you love me
if you do not want me to die,"
I am with my hand the goose in my breast
downbeating,
"there is nothing to do," I tell them,
"but to have grandchildren."

Tante Tina's Lament

Haenschen is a fool
and I am his mother,
Dear Lord, forgive us both.
Haenschen in the city
struts, like a chicken.
He is wearing a pink shirt
and plaid, big-bottomed hosen.
When he was little,
his bottom was like a zwieback.
His little buns I spanked
and how he crowed!

Now his tongue he wags at me
and thinks I am ignorant.
He says farmers have no brains,
they should all be businessmen.
He says farm girls don't know how to walk
and I a steak don't know how to barbecue.
Oh his heart is full of borscht,
and his words are like sour cream.
Don't called me Haenschen, he says.
My name is John.
Do I not know my son's name?
Did I not for six nights with my man Doft
about that name argue already yet?

On Wednesday night
the young people go to church.
They are platz eating and testimonies giving.
The girls have long golden hair.
Their cheeks are rosy from harvest
and dresses their knees cover.
When the young people together sing

it is heaven above and earth below
with sopranos and basses.

But my Haenschen
to the city goes, to dance.
He has a girl friend.
On her lips she has red grease gesmeared.
Her blond hair is cut and curled
and her knees are bare
like a young calf.
When they are dancing
their legs are noodles
and the music is a tractor.
The girl friend says it is not a shame
a woman her hair to be cutting.
She thinks Mennonites are like Hutterites
and has never heard of rollkuchen.
What good can come of that?

Haenschen says she is a modern girl.
He says we must speak Englisch to her
because she to the United Church goes.
He says Low German is a pile of manure.
Listen here, my little boy.
I will surround you with Low German.
I will piles of it to you be speaking.
Then you will know what Low German is!
Then you will remember
a mother's anger is a willow switch.

He does not listen.
We are poor, he says.
We do not know how people are money making.
He wants to be rich, like the Englische,
and from mannagruetze to save us all.

His heart is tight as a pfeffernuss.
His head is a piroshki
with fruit stuffed.

In the barn, the cats eat mice
and for milking time they are waiting.
When my man comes in
I serve him dinner on a china plate.
But my son does not know happiness.

On New Year's Eve
we go to church at night,
and on Easter
when the sun rises
we are singing praises.
Haenschen is at church by eleven
on Easter.
On New Year's Eve
he goes dancing.
He is not even coming the children to hear
on Christmas Eve.
When he was still a bursch
he was a wise man in the play.

Oh my son
my heart so heavy is
thick as glums.
If you come home
it will rise, light and sweet.
I will make you porzeltche for breakfast
and every morning the New Year
we will celebrate.

Haenschen's Success

(Poor Immigrant Makes Good)

"But alas for you who are rich!"
cried the old blue denims.
Having outgrown them
I stuck them into a paper bag
and took them to the Mennonite Relief Store.
The grey-haired clerk
crinkled them open like an old songbook.
"What have we here?" he sang.
I shrugged my shoulders.
An iron-on seat patch glared at me.
"You have had your time of happiness!"
it shouted.
"What was that?"
asked the old man, cupping his ear.
I headed for the door.
"Yes, I'm sure they'll bring someone
happiness," he said, checking the pockets.

Out on the street
my corduroys hugged me.
I thrust my palms into their pockets
and we held hams
all the way home.
That night, religiously,
I hung them like a prayer
in my closet.

The next day my bells and I
were out strolling and they whispered
snugging up against my thigh,
"You know, a man that has
really ought to have more,

don't you think?"
Well, it's not every day a man's pants
give him that kind of freedom!
We swung into a store
and before you could say Steinbach
Manitoba's Automobile City
there was a whole choir of cords
humming in my closet.

Now, when I the door swing open
in the morning
it's like a Hallelujah Chorus in cotton
singing me out into the day.
"Praise the Lord!" shouts the chorus.
"Thank you that we are not blue.
Thank you for this free country
where a man above his jeans can rise."
Thus, every day, scripture and my thighs
are fulfilled and I respond, "Dear Lord,
my heart pants for thee.
Hallelujah. Amen."

Haenschen's Complaint

I am a father
and Johnny is my fool
God help him.
He swaggers like an Indian
in striped coveralls
and heavy leather boots.
He shuffles like his feet are cast in bronze.
When he was just a tyke
he wore the finest shoes.
I've had them bronzed
and set above the fireplace.

His tongue is a hundred dollar check
written on a one dollar brain account.
He says businessmen have no heart,
they should all be farmers.
He says city girls are prissy
and don't know how to make yogurt.
His words to me are like yogurt,
sour and with his own goodness dripping.
Don't call me, he says, I'll call you.
How sweetly he used to call me Papa!
Now he thinks
his father is a lending agency—
interest free!

On Wednesday night
the young people meet at our house.
They drink Seven-Up and swim in the pool.
The girls keep their curls above the water.
They bat their eyelashes
and show off new ensembles.
Later, the boys bring out guitars

and Gospel choruses they sing,
bouncy and clean as newborn babies.

But my appleseed
goes traipsing off to barn dances.
He has a girl friend
who says hair spray is unnatural.
Her hair is long and straggly.
She wears bluejeans
with patches on the seat.
When they dance
they stomp their feet and whoop
like a bunch of farmers.
The girl friend thinks Mennonites
wear big black hats.
She says Hutterites are with it
and has never a *Hymn Sing* seen on TV
What kind of bringing up did she have?

Johnny says she is a modern girl.
He says we should be kind to her
because she's from Toronto.
He says education is for fools.
He should know: all the way
through college I sent him already yet,
the little wise guy.
Behind a barn I should have taken him
and with a textbook thrashed.
Then he would know what education is!

His ears are full of wax.
We are too rich, he says.
We don't know how to live right.
He wants us to be poor, like the Indians,
and save us all from income tax.

His heart, at every inconvenience, bleeds.
His head is like my mother's steak
too long in the gravy left.

On the patio
my English sheepdog chews a milkbone
and my wife reads
Future Shock.
But my son cannot find happiness.

On New Year's Eve
we have church people over
and on Easter
we donate chocolates
to the Sunday School.
Johnny has a protest march
on Easter morning.
On New Year's Eve
he dances with tree huggers.
He doesn't even come on Christmas Eve
to hear the kids!
When he still was wet behind the ears
he was a shepherd in the play.

Oh my boy
what do you know about the price of land?
the dirt-floored houses and potato soup
we struggled out of?
If you come home
I'll plant in the back lawn a garden.
Every weekend, you can be pulling thistles.
And I'll never once, God help me, mention money.

Tante Tina Tells a Bible Story

At the gate in Latvia
on the train the soldiers came.
At each seat they are stopping.
Papers, they are papers wanting.
And things. Where is that samovar from?
Did you steal it?
And then they are taking it.
Or they are saying, these papers are not right.
And then Fred Peters from the train must go
and Mrs. Peters and the girls they are weeping,
please please.
When they are by me standing
where I am with my brother Nick,
I am not anymore a little girl running.
A squeal there is, in my heart, a piglet
through the mud scrambling, my fear
everywhere splattering.
So, running away from home?
No mummy and daddy?
Why not here be staying? We can take care of you.
One of them is my cheek touching and laughing
but the other one, he is asking,
What are you reading.
I read the Bible. It is all.
I need no others.
Ah so many good books
you are not reading, they laugh.
One is me on the breasts touching.
So many good stories you are missing.
I am about Jael thinking, how she
her body used, to bring the enemy into her tent, even,
ja, how she a tent peg used his brains out to be poking,
how many stories these soldiers are not knowing.

And then we through the gate are.
Look, look said Nick, we are free.
But I the story am reading, about David
seeing Bathsheba in the bathroom.
And I am about the border guard thinking.
In Canada, I have heard, the Indians are tents having.
So, I am thinking, they must tent pegs have.
A safe country. I am thinking. A safe country.

Tante Tina's Christmas

Me it's not
what they want.
It's my stories.

Tell us how it was
they ask me, imagine
my boy Haenschen and his little Haenschen
not so long ago just a little knirps
but now already with an anhaengsel. These girls
don't like me to say it so,
like they are something hanging on, but with names like
Angela and Mary-Jean, what else can I think?
Such names aren't Mennonite, that's sure.
But I love them, ja, they're my Haenschens.
What can I tell?
So ist das Leben.

Christmas afternoon the boys still groan
from too much turkey and potatoes,
eat halvah and play knipsbrat
and the kids go out down the riverbank
tobogganing.
It's the same, like it was.
And before that, even,
Weinachtsabend, after the children's program
at church—you know little Haenschen
read a scripture this year?
Even with his hair so long
they let him read, praise God—even then,
before the plates for each child
under the tree go, we all sing
"Welchen Jubel, Welche Freude,"
so nothing new under the sun comes.

I get older only.

Now they want stories,
how I walked to school in snow,
they want Russlaenda stories
from Opa and Oma.
Once, I tell them, we didn't all think
we could save the world.
That the Lord's work was.
Now even the girls go to college,
and what is coming of that?
A world without porzeltche
is not worth saving, or zwieback at least,
or borscht and rollkuchen,
but what do they know of that?

Ja, well, one time the Machnovites, the bandits, ja,
they came to our house in the Molotschna.
Everyone they would kill, they said, but Mutti
had borscht in a big topf steaming
and the men when they must choose
between their guns and a spoon for the borscht,
every time the spoon wins.
The soldiers ate themselves full
and went away, so you see? The Lord provides.
Haenschen, he likes that story
but his anhaengsel is not so sure.

Then I tell them,
Well that was my weinachtswuensch,
where is yours, and Haenschen, you know,
living in that big house with an Englische frau
he can still say:
"Da war einmal ein Mann
Er hatte eine Pfann

Die Pfann war ihm zu heiss
So ging er auf das Eis," und so weiter,
so I am happy.
And little Haenschen the grandboy with the hair
he can sing with the guitar:
"Haenschen klein ging allein
in die weite Welt hinein . . ."

So there we sit in the grautestov, ja,
my Haenschen in his fancy shoes
and his Haenschen in blue jeans
and the girls with Englische names even.
Who would say we mennonitisch are?

How we think, even,
is all aufgemixed.
Big Haenschen has his head all full of Conservative,
and little Haenschen preaches the NDP,
but you can still see it,
it's the same, how they walk,
the real Mennonite way,
like bringing in the cows . . .
except maybe too much sometimes
what was once on the boots clinging
now from the tongue falls, ja?

Tante Tina Calls in to a Canadian Radio Talk Show

Hello? Is this the radio?
The talk-in show? Ja, it's me
Tina again. Like a pig this thing squeals.
Turn my radio down? Ja. Just a minute. OK.

Ja, now I think the Russian
invasion of Grenada—pardon?
Ja, I mean the American invasion
on Afghanistan no, ja,
you know what I mean,
like the British when they came to Manitoba
when Louis Riel was here.
That's when the Harry Dick family
from our village in Russia came
but then they went to Mexico, because here it was all
so Englisch, you know?
But now his children
are coming back. Better knacksaut here
I say, ha ha. Ja. Altona is the sunflower
capital of Canada. Harry Dick,
he was my mother's uncle.
Tante Kate, she stayed here.
Twelve children, she told Uncle Fritz,
I'm not dragging them to Fernheim
just so we can our tongues in Spanish be wagging.
But some, like the Peter Dicks,
they went too and liked it.
No, I don't think they went to Grenada.
But Harry Peters, when he left Russia,
he came through Afghanistan,
and his children are now missionaries in India.

Ja, OK, I'll be short.
What my idea is,

I think they should all come back
to Manitoba—pardon?
Ja, I don't care, the Russians, the Americans, the Harry Dicks,
whoever. My Tante Frieda, she's still in Russia,
at Alma Ata, and Lydia Franz's boy Fred,
he lives in America, in Fresno.
So you see?

OK, I have to go now.
The platz is burning.

Tante Tina Reflects on Maggie Thatcher

That woman, ach du lieber,
no sauce on her verenicke
she's got, that's what, too much
pasty dough and two percent milk.
She should come to saengerfest
and sing along with all the other old ladies.
"O that I had a thousand tongues"
she should like, ja?
not all this stuff of never giving in.
She gave in long ago.
To rest by Ronald Reagan on his horse
her mind was laid.
Kids, even, they have, runt weanlings with diaper pins
in their ears, a hopeless bunch,
rock throwers, pinches off the old dough ball herself,
left too long in the oven,
like geroestete zwieback.

Maggie herself,
she too is geroestet.
She needs dipping in some tea,
get those buns wet already yet,
a good immersion baptism, and then
confession: Lieben sie die Brueder?
Let her confess before the whole church
how she found the Lord
right here at Tina's place.
Let her confess how Tina sat her down
with paska and glums, Tina ladled
all that pluma moos out of her head,
gave her potatoes to think about,
where they come from, and eggs,
let her shovel some of that other stuff

the chickens make,
she makes so well herself,
gave her halvah just to keep the plumbing clear.
Let her confess how Tina made verenicke
and Jim Reimer himself made the sauce
so good the Lord would eat.

Ach, Mrs. Thatcher, come down to Altona.
Change your name: Magdalena Thiessen
is much nicer, ja?
Flop your buns down in the kitchen here.
Confess a little. It's good for the bunyans.
So bad the world can't be
there's no hope.
You just come down here to Tina's.
We'll get you back in shape.
Then we can do something
about those men.

Tante Tina Remembers Trudeau

Everyone is today Trudeau forgetting
or bad things about him saying
but I think he should come down to my place
in Altona. I will make him some borscht,
and rollkuchen with honey
from the Thiessen place in Beaver Lodge.

And we can talk.
I will even some French for him be trying,
and maybe he can speak some Low German.
More tongues we need in this place,
not fewer. My man Doft has told me once
I am Mr. Trudeau loving too much and
he thinks I would like to kiss him,
or to run away with him even.
Well, maybe it's true
and I am sad
because there are no more politicians
I am feeling like kissing.
He the last one was, ja?
When we first came to this country
the Liberals were letting us in.
And when I am old,
Mr. Trudeau has me a check given
for old age pension. No one has such a thing
heard before in Coaldale or Altona.

Now all the lazy people want only
to speak in one tongue
like before Babel, but the Lord knows
this is only for money-making good.
For the borscht, the more things go in
the better the eating.

Ah, ja, what do I know,
but when the Holy Spirit came
and everyone was in tongues speaking
they did not all babble the same,
they only understood each other.
Already each tongue
their own country wants,
like Manning and Parizeau, but they are small
people, with visions like a rooster.
For myself, I would rather into the new year
porzeltche with Trudeau be eating
than mannagruetze with Manning.

But no one listens to an old lady
anymore, ja? So when we each
are sitting alone, speaking to ourselves
in our own tongue, like Mr. Toews here in the home
who always into his soup mumbles,
maybe they will remember me,
and Mr. Trudeau even,
and they will see, even if a man sometimes
wrong is, it is good to have someone
around to be giving a kiss, ja?

How A Story Made Little Haenschen and Angela Get Married

I have one evening the news on the TV
been watching on the green sofa with Little Haenschen
and his anhaengsel Angela in her blue jeans,
and her flannel shirt with some buttons open.
Then he has me been telling how one time
when he was still just a little knirps
we were together TV watching,
when his mother and father out were,
I think Mr. Diefenbaker to hear.
On the TV we have the old Doukhobor women seen
up to the front of the political konference
walking, like Mennonites, one foot in front of
the other, like they think they are somewhere going,
and they are their dresses for Mr. Diefenbaker
off-taking. Oh so wass! Like big lumps
of zwieback dough, ja?
Such commotion!
So I am to Little Haenschen saying,
I would never such a thing do.
No Oma? No. Never.
Those women their dresses off to be taking
like that, in front of the politicians,
it is like pearls before swine throwing.

But I am not this remembering,
that I would such a thing say to Little Haenschen.
And when I have to the kitchen for tea gone
my memories up-to-waken,
and they are thinking I don't hear,
Angela is whispering,
Oh let me your buns be squeezing,
and you can inside my shirt down-slip
the smooth shell-belly

to the soft-bearded oyster,
and then your liquid pearls are outcoming, ja?
I think she is mocking, ja?
But then the next Christmas
they have been married. So wass.

Chicken Soup

At nighttime now I am reading a book Big Haenschen
has me given for Christmas: Chicken Soup for the Soul.
And I am thinking that singing is for the soul
good, but chicken soup is for the body,
and on Sunday we should together
be eating and this idea is me happy making.
Until in the morning I am remembering
that Big Haenschen is busy with Mary-Jean's family
and Katie is in Vancouver
and Frieda has to Mexico gone to help
the poor people.

So Little Haenschen and his Angela
have been coming because they are thinking
maybe to have chickens in the city
in their yard and they want to be learning
from the best cook.
So I am happy.

When you are chicken cooking,
I tell them, it is good the neighbours to be calling
over the fence. If you are dumplings making
there is always enough, like the widow
and Elijah.

The hen your grandboy can be snatching
by the leg with a long pole and a hook on the end.

He will her be dragging and squawking like Elsie Kliewer
singing descant on "What a Friend we Have in Jesus" through the dust.

Then Little Haenschen can both legs hold
and I her neck be stretching across the stump.

The grandboy's Angela is looking away
and her eyes covering when I the axe am lifting
and I tell her she can be praying but
I must my eyes keep open
so I am not my grandboy's arm ab-geschlachting
like happened with Pete Friesen once.

Then we can let the body
go around the yard gallivanting
the little red fountains
up-spritzing from where her head has been.
When the children still were little, even the girls,
they would laugh and laugh,
and when she wearies from this life
of running running always running,
we ker-plumpse her
into a Topf of boiling water.

After, we in the shade of the big maple tree are sitting
and can hymns be singing when we the feathers
are plucking out. Sometimes in the old days
Frieda was piano playing from the house
so we could hear. So nimm denn meine Hände, I liked.
But now, the grandkids are music in the ears plugging
and their heads bobbing like chickens
but I am nothing hearing except the ambulance,
sometimes, over by the old folk's home.

I am letting Little Haenschen and Angela pinch out
and pull the prickly pin feathers.
They have small fingers, just the right size
for feathers pinching.

When they were little
Haenschen and Frieda and even sometimes Katie played

with the skinny feet;
they pulled the muscle strings
from inside their shirt-sleeves,
screaming and laughing to make the fingers move
to scare the cousins from Winnipeg.

When I rinse off the skin
I am remembering how before Katie has off gelauffen
with one of the Hardware Rempel boys from Winkler
she could cut the neck and tie off the food tube,
and then pull out the insides.
She used to be liking that,
with the intestines to be playing, slipping them
through her fingers she said, like fat worms,
and finding the heart.

Now Little Haenschen helps me a little,
but his father Big Haenschen and Frieda and Katie—
they are too busy for visiting.

Frieda has told me that in another country
maybe Mexico, I think,
they are special soup making
from the chicken insides, but here the Englische
even the French ones
just throw this away, or maybe give to the dog.

I am putting the chicken then into a big Topf
with the neck, liver, and the heart,
and enough water adding so that she floats.
Then I sprinkle a teaspoon of salt into my hand
and brush it into the pot with my other hand.

When Little Haenschen is the table setting
I am Angela showing how dumplings to be mixing

with flour and milk, and some baking soda,
and then how to make
puffy pillows with the dough
on the hills of chicken above the water.

Then we have time
to call the neighbours again
and our hands to be washing,
and when they are coming in,
the George Hueberts
from church, with three children,
we can put a lid
on the pot just long enough
so I can be praying and the food blessing.

I am with a big Löffel
the chicken and dumplings
spooning into our old white plates
with the chips on the edge,
and fresh peas also from the garden.

And Little Haenschen the neck also likes to chew
like his Opa used to. If there were only Mennonites
and no Englische we could sing Praise God
from Whom All Blessings Flow
but these neighbours are United Church
even with Mennonite names,
and not singing so good.

After everyone has been home-going
and the yard is dark, the birds are even quiet,
I am thinking to myself that old Kernlied

Weißt du, wie viel Sternlein stehen
an dem blauen Himmelszelt?

Weißt du, wie viel Wolken gehen
weithin über alle Welt?

Ach, ja, I am my hands rubbing together
by the window, sitting and singing,
remembering that I must not be forgetting
the chickens to feed before
I am to sleep going.

Okay, I am now going,
Gott segne uns.

Tante Tina Out of Time

Little Haenschen reflects on his grandmother

I did not take a running fling
over the cliff's edge today,
over the wrinkled silk of the lake
into the pale blue air,
into the happy company
of buff-and-cinnamon-feathered cliff swallows
like soft clods of earth with wings
plummeting just for the thrill,
up-swooping at the wave-tips.

In this moment, Tina, my grandmother,
is not yet dead. She is not yet a heart on a little swing,
inside a cage of chicken bones,
draped in a white cotton nightgown,
wearing round glasses,
on the nursing home bed,
straining to let fly
with too many untold stories.
She is not yet a little girl hiding,
from the czar, from Stalin,
from her mother's supper call, from Fred Penner's
anxious, adolescent lust,
among the Molotschna gooseberry bushes.

In this moment, she is a young balsam fir
at the lip of an escarpment,
what comes out when the old limestone sighs,
a waxy, prickly green breath,
swaying in the slight offshore breeze,
tightly holding my hand.
Don't let go don't let go.

Into the space where I would leap
my wife Angela appears,
her body breathing, wet and supple,
through snug Spandex rock-climbing gear,
and my friend John,
smugly grinning, ear to ear.
Back on the trail,
they are giddy with tales
of this tiny handhold,
or that loose rock, the possibilities
of a sudden tumble.

Three steps behind,
palm over my nose, I'm
whiffing sweet balsamic fragrance.

Uncollected and New Poems

Our Green Future

Thanks to Nick Lindsay, Edisto Island carpenter-poet, union organizer, who taught me poetry as craft.

Under a blinding sun,
we dig in the DRC.
We unearth your green mirages,
your precious, your precious
tin and tantalum, tungsten, platinum,
palladium, copper, and zinc.
We excavate for nothing,
for your black ink on balance sheets,
for zero benefits.
We offer you, a sacrifice
to your future, our bodies.

We scrounge for bushmeat
behind the pits and shacks:
the fallen half-sick fruit bats, pouched rats,
hobbling duikers.
They offer us scant sustenance to build
your earthly paradise.
They offer us Ebola, Marburg, Lassa,
the rare-earth haemorrhagic viruses.
These also we will offer you,
for your hallucinated future.
Bloody tit for ratatat.

Your cracked-pot bosses are demanding
oligarchic equalizers, tariffs, walls:
these also we can build,
if you like, of brick and tangled wire,
if we can pass between the barbs
the bones and shreds of flesh—our dreams—
if you will take them.

Yes, if we feint weakness, we can do this.

If you demand a recall,
we will take back the flawed, discoloured,
hijacked world. In darkened sweatshops,
for your consuming satisfaction,
for misdirected threads and tags,
uneven seams, we can, in concentrated
stitch-by-stitch, create a wobbly patchwork flag,
one union sutured for the battlements.

Workers in a fractured world,
let us never rest
from wresting power from the simpli-firing bosses.
Let's shock them into stunned negotiations.
Let's strike for higher pay,
for isolation pay and danger pay—
for workers everywhere
in Mexico and China, in India, and Bangladesh, and Vietnam,
Detroit, New Mexico and Nunavut, West Nile and West Virginia,
for miners, steel workers, minors, sex workers, cleaners of pig barns,
chicken feed gleaners, strawberry pickers,
old women, their osteoporotic backs bent in the offal
of the slaughterhouse, let's strike
for benefits, for health and paid leave, sick leave, a cot to sleep on,
and leave to hug our children before dawn.

If in each other's power
we find the flint to strike,
to use the crackling forge of our unwavering
flames to write rare-earthly songs of solidarity,
to sing around the bonfires
of their vanity,
to keep us warm
against the chill

of other's othering night.

We are the workers,
of and in this blazing world.

We can do this.
We will.
Do this.

2024

Writing, a Life

They are springboks and gazelles
leggy, shimmering in the late afternoon sun
on the high veldt,
hair tousled like native grass
bodies giddily tense, any minute now
expecting a clench,
a floating release,
a landing on those hard little feet.

The old man shifts
on the park bench
in the naked
sun of the late afternoon.

He is writing a poem
about death.
His mind is a panic
of springboks and gazelles
leggy, shimmering in the unslaked afternoon sun
on the high veldt, expecting,
any second now,
an epiphany.

1997

Animalphabet Politics

Apishly,
bullishly
cowed, we
doggedly
egged on the
ferrets of twittering
gadflies who,
horsing around like
insectigenic
jackasses kicked the
kids of kindness out of us,
larking even as they
monkeyed brutishly around with
nightingales of beauty, truth, nursing
ovine dreams,
parroting slogans,
quailing before the legions of
rat-at-atle
snakes with viral-bearing
ticks, prickly as
urchins &
vulpinishly
weaselling their way into our
xerus erythropusly skitterish hearts &
yakkity yakked us into the devil's
zibeline embrace.

2022

How to Love Toronto with a Dead Raccoon

(A villanelle for a post mortem)

Keep your scalpel steady, your wits, keen.
Don double gloves, white coat, a mask.
Brush gently down the fur, look well, cut clean,

but not before nose, eyes, ears, anus, bones
are checked for oddities, lesions from life now past,
to keep your scalpel steady, wits on edge; lean

over while you check for footpad mutilation
of the kind induced by—what? Your diagnostic task
down-brushing fur, looking and cutting clean,

will take you on a journey down through skin
through sternum, to the heart, lungs, liver, guts, and, last,
not least, your scalpel, and your wits, still keen—

you cut the bony lid away, to see the brain
and now, inside your head, think of the map,
brush gently down the fur, cut clean,

remember how the rabies epidemic came
in trucks and woods, the city's fate in landscape cast,
so, steady scalpel, wits and love for life still keen,
brush gently down the fur, look well, cut clean.

2009

A Lamentation of Stone

My thistly thighs,
under the wind's silk
lips, sighed in defeat,
I waited, stupefied
prostrate in the thin air.
How many years
at his feet? How many?

They arrived quarrelling, men
without motorcycles, women without Bond,
with God, each other, their damned thirst.
The bearded one with the singed hair
stepped ahead, anxious already.
I held back, dizzy in the ululating
dry sea, wanting him now, now
there in the dry bed of the Zin.
A voice from somewhere in the heat
whispered, raise your staff, speak,
but don't touch the goods.
She is mine, all mine.
Only speak to her.

No, speaking won't cut it.
He only knows what we can do
and is afraid. He is a jealous, burning bush,
a Being who is Being.
I've waited too long for this.

Hesitating, weak with longing
and power, my gown shifting in the wind,
by the strength of his longing,
by the power of his staff
I drew him down,

and at his touch, the defiling moment,
the fount of waters, all those years,
on the verge, the soft red voice at the cleft
a watery moan at noon,
a stream a sigh.

Later, on a bleak mountain
he contemplated a forbidden
vista: grapevines, olive breasts,
the sticky hum of bee-children, our children
suckled among dark leaves,
weaned on the thrill of pillage.

Resplendent in their naked
unthinking thirst for blood
how the stones flew, free at last,
singing home to the place of broken skulls
which is love, such a lovely dance,
wine-splash and myrrh on rock.

Oh yes, I had that fling with Michelangelo,
his stiff fingers on my hips.
Loving the old rock with his chisel,
we created the boy
who killed ten thousands,
only one that mattered,
he knew how to love, his lust unchained,
and such a wonderful singer!

Old tree, old hole in the rock
call me what you will, the old whore
I am still here, willing to take, and give,
I raise a glass
to my love, to the earth engorged,

to your hand upon me,
such a hard place to be,
knowing your heart,
knowing what has become of us.

Your wrinkled belly,
how it aches.

One final time,
we are almost gone now
come, dance the old belly to belly
with me, here in the desert,
hot rock-bites on our bone-dry
bottoms, the old guy still whispering
of love and sacrifice.
I am, he knows,
just one of many worlds.

2002

The Woodcutter's Fireside Song

Between the stars, a fine dust
drifts, wafting after
universal whistling
woodsmen, fine fellows
felling planets, one-by-one.
One tree, they missed
one little tree, too spindly
for the fire, third from a sun,
sapling from seed from clefts in rock
in shallow seas,
the roots as fine as lace
rice noodles ascarids,
strong as a lover's clasp
around, into the small
of no-going-back
all through the heart of things
the tree, four billion rings
of equisetum, garlic root, and algae
songs of icthys, duckbills, equis
romance riding into the breeding sunset,
stems bending all around
orgasmic joy, the full girth sending up
the tree, a crowning hominidal glory
a crown of fine roosts, fluting beaks,
and fiddles, hardwood dancing floors, orchids of poetry,
and all that monkey business.

The old tree, so consumed with self
is open for business, bends over for business,
and with a sigh consumes himself,
his industrial pudding, his progress pie,
his orchids, nibbling down the trunk.
He is deep throat.

Now he has reached the balls of the matter
the heart of the matter
His lust insatiable, his pride in vain.
He is nibbling at the fine roots
with his little golden teeth.
He nips deliriously,
chops incisively
hacks lustily.
He whistles a missile tune.
He carries himself home
in chords between the stars.

In the small of his back,
and in what is wrecked
and left behind,
a requiem, caressing song,
a fine dust, a dark matter,
drifts and whispers.

2006

At Dusk, a Merchant

At dusk a merchant,
stumbling down the bloody way
from temple to the site
of fallen walls and slaughter,
was ambushed, beaten, left
for dead. Then came the scavengers:
first passed the one who, praising
heaven, tore from the body grace
to not have been this poor unfortunate;
then circled by a second who wrought beautiful,
holy laments from other's anguish.
A third, seeing a fellow traveller,
stopped, dressed their wounds,
and carried them to shelter.

The flustered innkeeper frowned
at the shivering heap
curled like a street dog
on the merchant's mat,
rubbed the silver coins
placed on the counter.
And where will you be?
I must head back across the river
before dawn, or I'll be killed.

The keeper, considering
the merchant's accent,
wondered if he should seek
a lawyer for advice on liability,
but, considering the time of day,
the cost of paying overtime,
the cost of living,
the cash in hand,

the price of mercy,
he relented.

That night
wrapped in time-torn shawls
and huddled on the stone-cold step
outside the door,
the keeper watched as clouds
were swept away, unveiling
bright-starred heavens,
clearing his anxious mind,
and, for the first time felt,
after a long and troubled life,
peace.

2023

Letter to an old PC: Das Re-boot

We took a walk down old drive C:\
one cool October eve.
We spoke of ones and zeroes
as my hands caressed your keys.

We walked the path less travelled.
I leaned close to your ear
and, all alone on a single track
I whispered softly, dir:/

I'd always loved your software,
basic, programmable.
I could feel it in my hardware
that we were compatible.

You held me off with, More, please wait,
and added, Please stand by.
I worried, then, searching your face
for just one Readme file.

Alas, it was too late, I feared;
the disk grew black and blacker,
as, weeping zeroes you confessed
you loved another hacker.

I held my rage as you retraced
that same DOS walk with me,
till, looking sadly at your face,
I typed in "Format C:"

1991

The Memories of Buildings

I. Kitchener

What does a 75-year-old house remember?

Scars, and remnants of what was there,
appendix, tonsils,
stretch marks.

This is the bedroom where your daughter
leapt from bed
the night the frozen pipes burst,
spraying a bouquet of ice monsters.
See, there, the scar in the closet;
and the windows from which you could hear
the mindless smash of beer bottles in the street,
the jetsam of ever-changing neighbours.

From your son's windows you can see the great
black walnut trees, the squirrels,
with their anxious, forgetful buryings,
the once-not-weedy tennis court.

Here in the hall is where the cat clawed through
three layers of antique wallpaper
and plaster.
This is the kitchen nook where teenaged legs
scuffled a space for themselves.

This was your old, dark study,
the bedroom with the Argentinian brass bed
with the bullet dents: immigrant memories,
like so many others, dragged here to remember,
now dislocated, lost

in the Canadian wilderness.

Ice and rocks, once.
Trees and a railway, not so long ago.

The neighbour is renovating.
Recovering her memories,
the neighbour's house talks to ours,
looking for confirmation:
Are these back stairs
right? These cornices?
Am I a false memory, made real,
a future recollection?

At night, the old house creaks in her dreams,
so many of her friends
now dancing to the rhythm
of a wrecker's ball.

Somewhere, an engineer
is dreaming better roads through the city,
is dreaming an Alzheimer's
city, fretful, forgetting itself,
is dreaming.

In the high branches of the black walnuts
the cardinals and mourning doves,
and in the attic eaves the squirrels,
are moving on
with life.

II. Kathmandu

Along the narrow lanes
from Durbar Square
down to the Bishnumati River,
the buildings lean,
their thousand-year-old thighs and bellies,
dusky brick; wrinkled, carved wood-latticed
balconies press, immodestly,
their cleavages into the crowd. Cracked,
weathered visages of old men
and gargoyles keep watch at cornices.
Inside, as morning sunbeam waifs
snuffle into dank, stone shade, child goddess queens
hold dust-bouquets
with baited breath.

They have seen all this before:
the scream of rock throwers,
anti-rock-throwers, motorcycles, diesel, plastic,
the spew of chamber pots and spit
the hacks of tuberculosis
and the computer trade,
all that wanting, wanting, wanting.

At dusk, wheezing, they sip
from fragile chalices of ice-water and moonlight.
Their thoughts slip into shadows,
wandering, dazed ducklings in the street-litter.
They know what is wanting. Above
the death-stench at their feet
a faint scent of pine and cardamom
lingers, a taste of warm yak milk
from the high valleys,
and green mangoes from the terai.

The skin-cracked buildings remember,
tongues and limbs still aching,
how they were built, muscle by muscle
like a morning stretch, half dozing,
from the green valley bed,
how they suckled vagabonds and despots,
their unabashed desire
echoing in rocks, moss,
snow palaces.
They whisper tales of gold,
azure, saffron, green,
of caves where monks dreamed themselves
into being, and out, blood in the streets a sacrifice
for something, somewhere,
perhaps along the mountain crowns:
glory, perhaps.

In early dawn, before
the yapping dogs and indigestion
of traffic, before the grey-water light
spills from satellite dishes
and floods down potholed roads,

a child comes, thin, shivering,
bent under a splintered splay of wood,
from the mountains, in tatters
of dazzling red and green
and shattered Himalayan ice-light,
gesturing for them to harken;
she comes to tell them
who and why they are:

they bend to listen.

Something, they hear, about forgetfulness,
and then her voice is trampled:
a tourist helicopter
whinges overhead, replete
with bored money-spenders,
to the gods' abode.

And in the street
a wedding band,
bang-thumping drums,
and wild, twisted blasts,
tramps past,
a trashy parody of New Orleans

or anthems to kings and gods long dead
Gurkhas or Sherpas regaling with fireside tales,
or some small, forgotten happiness,
a mother in a mountain village
a tree beside a clear stream,
a shaggy yak footing the stony path,
birds screaming overhead.

The old buildings tremble.
In their wooden bones
and feet of clay, in a long
hacking clearing of the lungs, they exhale,
and remember.

2007

The Way of Memories

All that I have met is part of me
carried down secret corridors,
electric passageways, down mysterious
axon elevators, packed
in molecules of RNA,
stored in grey salt mines of cerebral cortex
like radioactive waste.
What is the half-life of memories?
Somewhere my childhood is decomposing,
disintegrating into simpler, more stable forms
beyond the reach of even the most skilful miner,
the most dextrous neurosurgeon.

When the aeons of decay are over
the memories, no longer hot,
are shipped in protein submarines
along the tropical rivers of blood,
dumped in the liver for a final detoxification.

Surely, I shall die of obstructive jaundice,
my common bile duct clogged, painfully,
with calculi of memories.
In the final moment they will dissolve
and I shall remember everything.

1973

The Fat Lady Struck Dumb

It ain't over till the fat lady sings

A soft swarm of lost voices, like rare, muffled pink
pigeons, rumples the smooth summer air:
sighs of Spanish, chortled slav-tongues, warbled
Englishes of England, Jamaica, India,
the grackled Frenches of Quebec, Haiti, Algeria, Paris,
Hindis of Vancouver, London, Delhi,
Arabics of Sudan, Somalia, Jordan;
the trees tremble with the flap and squabble
of a thousand sausages with sauerkraut,
empañadas flocking and swooping,
and fluttering scents
of salsa, cinnamon and baklava.

In Victoria Park, City of Kitchener,
Victoria Day, beneath the statue of Queen Victoria,
the Empire of the Dispossessed
strikes back.

Still, I stand amid chill
airstreams they have surfed to come here,
ragged winds filling sails of union jacks
fleur de lis stars stripes crosses crescents,
the snarling
downdrafts of nationhood.
They have come for dancing, justice,
fresh pastry, a kiss on the cheek,
a decent job, no guns at the grocery store.
They have come to circle the statue of the fat lady,
to drape her with a lacy shawl of droppings.
They have come to nest
nibble scratch poke together a new place,
a new country, another world.

The prickly grass of home puckers at our bare soles,
welcomes us with a big open-mouthed kiss,
loving us, devouring us,
bringing us into the old Canadian family.
Singing above, we are joined
from below by our country's founders, a vast, Wagnerian
harmony tongue-tickling our arches,
la-di-da-ing at our backs, tum-tiddling our bones,
humming in the stem cells at the marrow's heart,
twisting in the ancient codes
that make us
who we are: the Auruch, the Quagga,
Gypsonia, Dickinsonia, Glyptodont,
the Moa, the Ammonites, the Trilobites,
the chorus bursting through us, from us,
poetry of the Burgess Shale and the Skeleton Coast,
trios of Leaky's Lucy, Java Man,
and my grandmother:
here we come, the Canadian Valkyrie eleisons
singing as we tumble,
tongue to tongue,
a giant wave roaring and hissing head over heels
across time's shifting strand.

Before us, mouth gaping, swept up, uprooted
in our uproarious tide,
the fat lady, once puffed up with
gall and bold pronouncements
on her pedestal, now helpless as the flightless kakapo,
is struck
dumb.

How the Earth Loves You

One day, perhaps when you are
in your forties, he is at your door
with a spring of daffodils.
Another day he bears lilies,
or jack-in-the-pulpits,
every day a flutter of fresh petals
and another scent whispering
at the skirt of your hair.
He seems disconcertingly traditional.
He brings roses, for instance, red ones.
You are bemused.
You look past him, sheepishly,
to the shapes of clouds,
to the paling blue sky.
When your eyes return from flight
you see your hand is bleeding,
you are clutching a sprig of thorns,
and he is gone.

He returns with fat red tomatoes,
waxy green peppers, a peach pressed firmly,
gently, from his palm to yours.
You can still feel the scars
from his roses. Your hand retreats.
Your fingers brush.
Your breath like a wave curls under, tumbles,
pulls back. Your belly tenses.
You are surfing, barely skimming the sand,
an unspeakable fear swelling your tongue.

Do not speak it.
This is what you were made for,
the heat of his gaze on your forearm,

burning your cheek.
You feel the slack first in your knees,
then your back. Do not succumb.
The best is still to come.

In the fall, he leaves in a glorious swirl
of gold and rust, amid the chatty travel songs
of migrating birds. You ache in his absence,
raking at the unreachable pain
in your chest. When you think of him,
you balk at his easy certainty,
his knowledge of your desire.
You delight in the melting snowflakes
that catch in his hair.
You sigh at how his breathing undulates
under the white quilt. It is enough to lie
in bed on a slow Saturday,
to know he will come, his cool palm
stroking your belly, your breasts,
unexpectedly clutching your breath
as if it were another bouquet.

Do not hasten his wooing.
He will come soon enough.
You must not speak his name.
Only when you slip life's pearls
through your fingers, like a rosary,
counting the day after day
of his unfailing courtship,
when you have ached for him
in all the little things—in how you walk,
how your fingers probe a place for seeds,
how your cheek presses to his hard belly,
how you touch the mound where new life stirs—
only then will you be ready,

the light will break through
and the darkness, together,
and you will understand, finally,
who it is who has loved you
all this time, so well.

AFTERWORD

Writing as Immersion Baptism

David Waltner-Toews

I come from a religious tradition where the only true baptism includes having your full body submerged until you feel as if you're drowning, and then being lifted back up into your new, radiant life. This afterword is an account of a few of the many baptisms I've experienced. I am still, after more than seventy years, struggling with a life of breathlessness, and, occasionally, radiance.

Aside from a brief period where I aspired to be a cowboy missionary, I have always wanted to be a writer. Poetry is a thread that stitches my patchwork life together. If you pull the thread, I may fall apart completely or be left wearing the emperor's new clothes.

The first poem I remember writing was when my grade 5 teacher asked me to write a poem as punishment for talking in class. How did she know I was even interested (in poetry, I mean, not punishment)? It was near Christmas. I wrote something that rhymed, probably in iambic pentameter, about wise men, a kind of upbeat version of T.S. Eliot. Had I read T.S. Eliot? I don't remember. The teacher liked the poem so well that it was published in a Manitoba Teacher's Society journal and read on CFAM, Radio Altona. At least that's my recollection, although I've never been able to verify this. Poetry as punishment and glory: it is something I have wrestled with my whole life.

As a teenager, I was a true believer, and my writing reflected that—angry at the world, full of judgement. I wrote a lot of letters to the editor of the *Mennonite Brethren Herald*. I wrote a long poetic tirade, "A Brotherly Philippic," which was included in a book of essays called *Out of Concern for the Church* (Toronto: Wedge Publishing, 1970), a publication of Reformed Church Christian activists and scholars. It is the first and only piece of my writing that I registered with the Canadian Copyright Office—under the pseudonym D.T. Ivanovitch (David Toews, son of John, the Russian version, in case you wondered). What was I thinking? That someone would steal this?

Also, writing for me has never been just about writing. It has had to be good for something. What was the point of writing? At first, besides writing for self-punishment, I wrote for individual people and specific occasions—birthdays, Mother's Day, funerals, anniversaries, crushes. It was a cheap present that didn't require me to go shopping.

My 1966 high school valedictory address was a long poem. It was published in the *Mennonite Brethren Herald* and resulted in my first cheque, for two dollars, which I never cashed. Also in 1966, a letter from another *MB Herald* reader advised that the passage 2 Peter 2.12 should be applied to me. For those who don't know their Bibles so well, verse 12 is: "But these, as natural brute beasts, speak evil of the things that they understand not; and shall utterly perish in their own corruption."

Writing as glory and punishment.

January 19, 1967, my first short story was published in *The Uniter*, the student paper of United College, which later that year became the University of Winnipeg. It was titled "A Helping Hand," and is a sad tale about a Saint Bernard dog. He saved a girl's life, and is left abandoned and dying in the streets of Winnipeg. He is subsequently killed by a truck and is taken away by the garbage men. At the time, the idea that I might someday become a veterinarian was not even a vague fantasy. My high school English teacher predicted, at a graduation banquet, that I would one day teach history at a Bible college.

As a teenager, I walked down frozen windswept streets, reprimanding myself with Hamlin Garland's "Do You Fear the Wind." I lived in Winnipeg. Garland understood this desire to walk across Portage and Main in January and "walk like a man!" I thought maybe poetry, like a metaphoric buffalo coat, would get me there. In my writing I veered wildly between the extremes of sentimental greeting card rhymes, composed for birthdays, funerals, and other similar occasions, and raging, out-of-control laments, which might or might not have been therapeutic. In my first year of university, 1966-67, my poetic muses spoke to me in the reckless Pentecostal tongues of Dylan Thomas, the sly, learned seductions of John Donne, the upside-down judgements of William Blake, the moonlit wanderings of Byron. I wrote poems and stuck them into essays for courses in political science and history and literature, as if, by putting them into a serious context, I could redeem both the poetry and the essay. The professorial response was decidedly mixed.

In 1967, I was out-maneuvered on all fronts. Cultural upheaval was happening everywhere but Winnipeg. Our family, like a dandelion puffball, scattered. My oldest sister had already gone to teach in Africa. My only brother had a full scholarship to Harvard. My Dad quit his job in Winnipeg and my parents left home for Europe. From what I recall, as a self-absorbed teenager, the college where he had worked for twenty years, and been president for seven, never publicly recognized that he had been there nor that he was leaving. Rumour had it that they were afraid that if applicants knew my dad left, they might not apply. It left me with a lifelong distrust of institutions, and a vow that I would never be a university professor.

What was left for me to do? Being from Winnipeg, how could I be a rebellious 1960s teenager? Go to San Francisco? To the Chelsea Hotel? I was not so brave nor so reckless. Canadian Prime Minister Pierre Trudeau said we should do something for our country. I worked a few months for a factory making cement curbs, then dropped out of university after a year and hitchhiked to Montreal, where for two dollars a night, I slept in a cubicle in a Czech mission, and wandered around Expo '67. In a spasm of Mennonite naïveté, I posed nude for a local sculptor, imagining myself as Michelangelo's David. I took a freighter to Belfast, and then just kept going. This was my gift to Canada.

I hiked around much of Ireland. My journal specifically mentions Brendan Behan, whom I don't recall ever reading. Why not Yeats or Joyce? I must have been overwhelmed by teenaged hormones and fresh Irish air.

From Dublin, I took a ferry to Wales, where I slept in a churchyard, then hitched rides to London. I saw a lot of stage plays, including *The Merchant of Venice*, *Little Murders* by Jules Feiffer, and Strindberg's *Dance of Death*, with Laurence Olivier in a leading role. I got his autograph. In my journal I noted that the play and Olivier's autograph "converted me." To what I did not say. Later I added, "Drama and literature are my life." When I realized I was using all my scant money to see a lot of plays, I headed north to Scotland, looked around, climbed a hill, bought a sweater, saw a play, and headed back to London.

In London I met a girl from California. She said her name was Melody Papini. That didn't sound like a real name to me. A fantasy. She needed a guy to hitchhike with across Europe and picked me out of a crowd at a London Youth Hostel. She was heading south, to Italy, I think. At the time, I thought she liked me in some romantic way. I'd read Byron, after all. I was bedazzled. Later, I realized that, being a girl on her own, she was looking for safety. She left me in Germany when she realized that I might be a religious romantic with parental issues, writing sentimental poetry. I thought I might go to the Greek Islands, where everyone else seemed to be going, but a tiny Soviet-built car full of happily inebriated Yugoslavs took me instead to the coastal town of Rijeka, in what is now Croatia. After a night of sleeping among rocks and thorns beside the road, followed by a few other random rides with friendly strangers, I got picked up by a Ken Kesey-type school bus going to Istanbul.

In Istanbul, I met a group of travelers who were riding in the back of a British surplus military truck. For almost all the money I had left, they would take me overland to Kathmandu. I had heard of Istanbul, which was exotic and had something to do with Christianity becoming a state religion, but Nepal and India were off the edge of the planet. I had no idea what was between here and there. I had no money for a return trip.

There were: markets (the real ones, not the virtual gambling casinos we call stock markets), the Mediterranean, deserts, ruins of crusaders and Persians, vaccines given with reusable needles in hallways in a dirty Tehran hospital, a dash out of a Tehran Hilton with rolls of toilet paper under my shirt, a non-Beatle haircut requirement at the Afghan border, hundreds of miles of bumpy Russian-built concrete road (Herat to Kandahar), hundreds of miles of American-built smooth tarmac (Kandahar to Kabul), a ghostly, empty luxury hotel in the rocky desert where the two roads met, and welcomes into homes for tea, or rice and curry, or shops to change money where the boy ran out the back door and disappeared with your travelers' checks. There was also this: the sense that the European and American literature I so loved was a smug, self-congratulatory Empire Club, oblivious to its own insularity, a little like me.

When, in Persia, at the tomb of Darius, I stood in the sand intoning Shelley's "Ozymandias," I might have been pronouncing a dour homily on all that I once believed and held dear and was now a "colossal wreck" with the "lone and level" steppes stretching in all directions.

Everywhere on my journeys, I was taken in by families who fed me, gave me a place to sleep, and generally treated me, a stranger, with great generosity and kindness. I had been led to understand that non-Christians were going to hell. I had believed it. But what to do with all these kind and generous people?

Everything I had grown up with seemed tainted by bullshit, in the sense that philosopher Harry G. Frankfurt uses it in his little book of the same name. That is, not a lie, but verbiage indifferent to truth.

Now, in a state of shock, nihilistic depression, and awe, I had to figure out the meaning of life from scratch. If I couldn't trust the teachings of my childhood, taught by people who had gained a state of unassailable righteousness by surviving the Russian Revolution, then I couldn't trust anyone, or any system where idea trumped evidence. I worried that any religious or political ideology was tainted by bullshit, even as I tried them all on for size.

By late December 1967, in the blazingly hot, overcrowded, filthy streets of Calcutta, I was running out of money. I was also running out in other ways; at one point my uncontrollable diarrhea could only be relieved by stepping into a narrow side street, and, like any other human in that place, pulling down my pants and letting it all out. Squatting there, I was both humiliated, and, in some small way, sent on the beginnings of a journey to claim my place as a member of the human species.

Revolted by white kids panhandling in India, humbled by the limits of my body and wits, I found the Mennonite Central Committee office and wandered in, looking for work. They were skeptical of a scruffy-looking kid with an Army-Navy backpack. But the director had been to the Bible college in Winnipeg where my father had taught. I could scoff at the international Menno-mafia, but I wasn't stupid. MCC needed someone to fill in until an

American volunteer could get visa clearance. So I became an expert in rural development, hopped a train for Bihar, and spent my first night sleeping on the floor of a bookstore, brushing away the rats that nibbled at my ears.

Bihar, which seemed to me a wasteland of poverty, drought, and hopelessness, is also home to the Bodhi tree ("tree of awakening"), under which Buddha is said to have achieved enlightenment. My job lasted six months. I did not achieve enlightenment. I fell into a fog which has followed me my whole life.

After that job in poverty-stricken Bihar, in July of 1968, in the midst of some of my darkest hours, I took comfort in a ratty copy of *Gitanjali*, or *Song Offerings*, by the Nobel-prize-winning Bengali poet Rabindranath Tagore, with a mystical, quasi-erotic preface by W.B. Yeats. I had picked it up at a street vendor in Calcutta. I carried it with me everywhere. Once, book in hand, I sat staring out to sea on a wide, hazy beach south of Orissa. A businessman from Calcutta, walking past in his suit, barefoot in the sand, saw what I held in my hand. He asked if I knew the melodies to these songs. I said that I did not. He sat next to me, closed his eyes, and sang several of the songs to me, and then continued on his way. It was a small gift, one human to another. I wanted to write poetry like that.

I met a group of French students who asked me what I was doing in Asia. I explained that I was a vagabond and a writer. They thought this was romantic. I was lost.

In 1969, exhausted from my travels followed by six months working in a sawmill in Vancouver to pay off debts and save some money, I went to Goshen College. They offered to give me a year of university credit for my grade twelve, plus another year for my one year at United College, plus they had a program called Study Service Trimester (SST), which meant I could spend a semester in the French West Indies, immersed in French. So, a four-year degree based on a year-and-a-half of coursework. For a confused twenty-year-old, what was not to like? Plus, it was a Mennonite school, which might keep my parents, if not happy, at least satisfied.

My poetry instructor at Goshen was Nick Lindsay, son of Vachel Lindsay, the founder of what he called "modern singing poetry," which is one version of performance poetry. Nick, who carried on the tradition of poetry as singing and chanting, was a carpenter from Edisto Island,

South Carolina, as well as a poet. I found Lindsay's chanting, hypnotic incantations puzzling in their points of reference, embarrassing in their raw emotion, and inspiring for their unabashed chutzpah. In some ways, this chanting poetry was perfect for what I wanted: poetry that was directly engaged with what people did every day in their working lives, and which performed better on the stage than on the page. At the same time, I wasn't quite sure how to translate that into something usable in my own writing. I focused, then, on the daily drills Nick required of us, writing in various poetic forms, learning basic structures and techniques. One summer, as a kind of discipline, I wrote a sonnet every day, like Hannon exercises and scales for the piano. By the end of the summer, I had reduced the definition of sonnets from Petrarchan and Shakespearean to, well, fourteen lines. Giacometti sonnets, one word to a line. Look at them askance and they disappear, like the angels that may have visited my childhood bedroom. Sonnets about nothing.

But apart from personal therapy, to what end all this writing? After the Bihar experience, what could a person say that was not futile, wearisome, so world-weary that a man would have nothing to say? All was vanity. That fall, just after arriving at Goshen, I initiated an exchange of letters with Jack Dueck, one of the profs at Goshen, and apparently (I discovered more than fifty years later) somehow related to me, that Mennonite thing again. If the universe had no meaning, I argued, then writing was pointless. Which meant that I myself, being a writer, was of no consequence. I told Jack that "my writing [since of course I could not stop, even though it was pointless] exhibited desperate silliness. Giggling in the face of disaster. Hallucinatory . . ." The poems I wrote while at Goshen were absurd, full of death, judgement, and hopelessness.

I was rescued, lifted up out of the suffocating water of the baptism dunk, by two other professors, Mary Oyer and Mary Eleanor Bender. From Oyer, I learned history of European music, arts and western civilization. Mary Eleanor Bender taught courses in French Language and Literature, as well as twentieth century fiction from Europe and the Americas—writers like Sartre, Camus, Mann, Beckett, Ionesco, Kafka, Wolfe, Mansfield, Woolf, Joyce, Bernanos, and Robbe-Grillet. At some point in the course, she leaned over the podium and spoke quietly to us, to me specifically, I thought, and said, "They have defined the problem. Now it is up to you to find the solution."

This was my Great Commission. But how would I even begin when all those great minds had already foundered on the dark shoals of World War? I still wrote obsessively every day, but at least now, when someone asked why, I didn't have to stop at "because." I was working in the Kingdom of God, along with the Berrigan Brothers, Bob Dylan, Denise Levertov, Leonard Cohen, and Lawrence Ferlinghetti.

At the time, with the world around us falling apart, writing seemed like a pointless distraction from real action. I was learning from Lindsay how to handle hammers, nails, chisels, saws, how to build poems, but who would live in them? It was only much later, decades after leaving the quarrelsome cosiness of liberal arts academia for a paying job in the dung-and-disease business that I realized how fortunate I had been to have had a carpenter as a poetry teacher.

In the winter of 1970, my daily journal from Guadeloupe, where I was immersed in French-Caribbean island culture, was a folio of poems and paintings. I wrote many songs, and, accompanying myself on a classical guitar, recorded them with an old-style reel-to-reel tape recorder. I suppose I wanted to be Leonard Cohen. That same winter in a 1970 letter to me (note my birth name) the Canadian Mennonite novelist Rudy Wiebe wrote: "A double-fisted kiss (Russian style) of congratulations to David Toews . . . He writes with his head and his gut—and he is beginning to hate well." Did he think these words would spur me on, encourage me?

While at Goshen, after flirting with Zen Buddhism, and studying the music and art of John Cage, Robert Rauschenberg, and Jean Tinguely, I put together a collection of my writings called *Again the Enemy Soldiers: a terminal artgame*, or, alternatively, *Non Cents and Other Rates of Exchange*. Nick Lindsay's comments on my work were that "I think it's delightful. But of course I think it's a lot of rubbish." To which, privately, I responded with a quote from Dostoyevsky's *Brothers Karamazov*.

"Poetry is rubbish!" said Smerdyakov curtly.
"Oh no, I am very fond of poetry."
"So far as it is poetry, it's essential rubbish."

I took all this to heart, but kept writing. It is a life-long, incurable addiction.

Nick Lindsay incited us to write, whether we believed in it or not, and Goshen's Pinchpenny Press seduced us with promises of publication. For a time, I edited a student paper, *The Other Wall*. I have no idea what the first wall was.

Nick Lindsay's influence—and that of his father, the former poet laureate of Seattle—was palpable in the forms of my writing, the chanting rhythms and public performance. One poem from that time, "Animal Farm Comes to America" (published in *Thirteen Poets*, Pinchpenny Press, 1971), begins

The streets rumble under the thundering herds
Flee to the mountains; crouch in caves.

and ends by announcing

Flee with your heart and shirt undone
Flee to the mountains; crouch in caves.
For Circe who turns men to swine has come,
And the world wallows down to the open graves.

In 1970, I wrote some poems under the pen name Cherain, which may have been a Freudian misreading of Chiron, the Centaur wounded by Hercules, and inventor of emergency and trauma medicine. Veterinary medicine was still not anywhere on the list of things I might want to do with my life. One of the Cherain poems, "Circus Animal," was later renamed and included in my very first collection, *That Inescapable Animal* (Pinchpenny, 1974). In it, I announced that

Every man must now play clown or beast
and even the Midwestern rocking chair is in the ring

and

Laughing free in the streets, the poet has escaped his lair.

In the late twentieth century, the term "performance poetry" was used (some might say co-opted) by certain poets to demonstrate their originality, this quality being elevated to the realm of the sacred. Performance poetry of course has a long tradition which predates written books, winding its way through oral histories and storytelling of many cultures, from Homer to dub. This sort of poetry has drifted into and out of popularity, and often marginalized from mainstream literature into such poetry ghettoes as Caribbean dub or American rap. In 2021, performance poetry jumped into the cultural mainstream with Amanda Gorman's performance of "The Hill We Climb" at the US presidential inauguration. Even then, one could hear critics mutter that this wasn't real poetry. Probably the same earnest self-appointed literary critics who scorned Bob Dylan's 2016 Nobel Prize for Literature.

In 1971, I graduated with a cobbled-together four-year literature degree, which included courses on German and French language and literature, as well as British, American, and modern Chinese literature. I skipped my graduation ceremony to marry Kathy Waltner, my life-guide, debater, challenger, ground-truther, and humblifier. Needing to stay in the US until Kathy finished her nursing degree, I worked for a small fanatically conservative religious publisher in layout and design, wrote an incredibly boring novel, watched Mutual of Omaha's *Wild Kingdom*, and wondered what I would do with the rest of my life. With my Bihar enlightenment trailing after me like a dark dust cloud, like Pig-Pen in the cartoon strip *Peanuts*, I needed to do something that was useful, real, engaged with life. Also, I needed to make a living.

I considered graduate studies in comparative literature, but I didn't want to be a writer who wrote about, and analyzed, other writers. I wanted to write about "real life." But what was that, even? I still had it in my mind that I did not want to be an academic.

Veterinary medicine, I thought, might help me. In 1972 I started studying science courses, with a view to becoming a veterinarian. That would be practical. I might even be able to make a living. Even if I never wrote another word, I could do something useful in the world. But of course, I could never not write another word.

In 1973, *The American Journal of Nursing* published my poem, "The Way of Memories," in which, for the first time, I scavenged medical metaphors and announced that

> Sure, I shall die of obstructive jaundice,
> my common bile duct clogged, painfully,
> with calculi of memories.
> In the final moment they will dissolve
> and I shall remember everything.

(As an aside, thirty years later, I returned to a similar theme, with a less sanguine ending, in which the "sanitary dream engineers" clear out my memories and dreams on a daily basis. Those of us of a certain age can relate to this.)

In the mid 1970s, while in veterinary college, I wrote a second novel: *The Sasquatch Memorandum, by Ima Buffalo*. It was a farce about Western Canadian separatist movements with links to Quebec separatism. An editor at a Toronto publisher liked it, but said that the topic was too timely, and wouldn't be of interest by the time the book came out. It was a lesson, once again, about the multiple solitudes that are Canada.

In Saskatoon, I continued to write every day, mostly poetry, and joined a small poets' support group—sort of like AA, but that served the opposite purpose of encouraging our addictions. The group included, among others, poet Anne Szumigalski, magazine editor Caroline Heath, and writer Mark Abley.

In 1976, between my second and third years at veterinary college, based in part on a reference from Rudy Wiebe, I applied for and received a Canada Council grant to write short stories. I read and re-read Philip Roth's *Goodbye, Columbus* to figure out how one might do that, and started what 30 years later would become the connected short story collection *One Foot in Heaven*.

After graduation with a DVM from University of Saskatchewan, I took my first veterinary job in Grand Prairie, Alberta. I was thirty years old. I had thought *One Foot in Heaven* might become a novel, but being in veterinary practice, a sole breadwinner with my wife and two small children at home, I didn't have time to write anything long-ish. I wrote lots of short poems about babies and housework and animals. I cobbled together my first real book of poetry, *The Earth is One Body*, and, shamelessly using my connections with the Saskatoon poetry group, persuaded the newly-established Turnstone Press in Winnipeg to publish it. The dedication on that book read:

> when I cook the borscht
> it is not because I love my wife
> when I scrub the floor
> I am not helping out the little woman
> I do not wash the dishes out of generosity
> I live here too

Turnstone also published my second book, titled, appropriately, *Good Housekeeping*, which included some poems by a new voice, Tante Tina.

Until that time, I had never written anything creative with the word Mennonite in it. But, without stirring up all the anger and angst and cynicism that I felt toward the institutions of my upbringing, could I do this? I knew it would need to have food in it. And, since the real history of Mennonites was best told by women in the kitchen and not the historians in the archives, that the voice would need to be female. My mother and her sisters, who had arrived as teenaged orphans from the USSR in 1926, were obvious role models. In the end, I was saved by a long poem from Uganda, introduced to me by Mary Oyer through Kathy, who had taken an African Arts course as a side to her nursing studies. Okot p'Bitek wrote *Song of Lawino* in 1966. He wrote in Luo, a decidedly non-mainstream African language, and it was translated, warts and all, directly into English. He called his style "comic singing."

Dancer, drummer, anthropologist, and social critic, he sang recklessly, full of love and therefore without self-censoring his deepest feelings, about the woes of modernization, of men running off to the big city, running after big city women and taking on big city airs, about corruption and infidelity and salvation, a song full of nostalgia, anger, hope, and, what was this—humour? I devoured the book-length tale-telling song at a sitting. That was me. That was my mother. Straight from Low German, the Mennonite version of Luo, into English.

And that voice became Tante Tina, straight into mangled southern Manitoba Mennonite English. She was my poetic voice for a decade, the 1980s, when many men were getting self-censored laryngitis. How could a white middle-class male with all the privileges and rights thereto attending have anything important to say at all? How could we get drunk and be miserable and happy without being accused, again, of some form of wrong-thinking or inappropriate feeling?

So I did the only thing I could: I got out of myself, sex change and all. I became an older woman.

My first "real Mennonite" poems, "Tante Tina's Lament," "Haenschen's Blues," and "Wald Heim," were published in a Toronto magazine, *Canadian Forum*, in about 1979. I laughed at the illustrations when the poems appeared in *Canadian Forum*, which were of Old Order Mennonites in black hats and kerchiefs: nothing at all like the Mennonites Tante Tina was talking about. A whole other tribe. Another sign, to me, that every label—Mennonite, Christian, socialist, scientist, poet—is both an opportunity and a trap, that every boundary we draw around ourselves is both necessary and is necessarily renegotiated day by day, fragile, temporary, not to be confused with reality, and usually misinterpreted by those around us.

Along with Kathy, our young children, and the cow poop and blood of my daily work, Tante Tina grounded me in ways that I had not been before. Tante Tina gave me a voice. Did I appropriate that voice? More accurately, I would say she appropriated me. I am, after all, the one who puts on the dress and babushka to wag my finger about Trudeau, Salman Rushdie, and the incorrigible stubbornness of Mennonite men. I am the one who loses my sanity and my rational epidemiological voice when she possesses me.

I have performed Tina in places where I, speaking as myself, would never have been invited. She was invited to speak at several conferences of an economic development agency, whose members include successful businessmen with whom I have, over the years, had some combative differences of opinion. One year Tina, in full costume, shared a stage in a barn in Altona, Manitoba (the alleged hometown of this fictional character) with a very serious Roland Penner, whose parents were among the founders of the Communist Party of Canada. I think he was ambivalent about sharing the stage with a Mennonite poet in drag, fearing perhaps that his own story might not be taken with sufficient sobriety of mind. This is a common misconception of course, that serious topics always require earnestness.

I was welcomed into churches, bars, synagogues, libraries, and on national radio. I recently received a letter from a former student who had seen me perform as a professor in a course on ecosystem approaches to human health. The performance had been in a bar. The student recalled that performance where, for him, I demonstrated that poetry and arts had important roles in conversations about health and environment. He subsequently stepped into a role as a Senior Indigenous Affairs Advisor for a national agency funding natural sciences and engineering research in Canada. Based on his grounded focus in that role, he is now studying to be a negotiator.

But I was not the character I played. How could I find my own voice? The mix of literature and veterinary medicine kept me sufficiently off-balance that I could never aspire to that great Mennonite goal—pride in humility. It also helped me keep a sense of humour. In 1983 after a conference at the Mennonite Center in Intercourse, PA, I received a letter that said, "your writings were so delightful I found my interest caught from the beginning . . . Incidentally, do you treat hogs . . . we could use a good hog vet."

In 1984, when Larry Danielson wrote and put on a stage adaptation of my poems in Morden, I understood that there might even be a space for my voice somewhere in Southern Manitoba. "Roots," the poem about Rudy Wiebe (which claims not to be about Rudy Wiebe), I am told, got the biggest applause. I don't know what that means. I could read into that something about the necessary overthrowing of the elders, but I am getting too far along myself to go down that road.

In 1986, when we were in Indonesia, I attended a conference in Singapore of the Commonwealth Language and Literature Association titled: "Englishes of the Commonwealth." I performed Tante Tina, and made an immediate connection with the British-Guyanese writer David Dabydeen, who said his own grandmother would tell the same stories, with their own unique brand of English.

That same year, I got a handwritten letter from my high school religion teacher (not the aforementioned English teacher). I had always remembered him as one of the bad guys, from whom I'd learned that everyone who was not a Christian was going to burn in hell. His father was dying, and he had picked up my collection of poems, *Good Housekeeping,* in which I had poured out my feelings at my own father's death. He wrote to thank me, as it resonated deeply with him. He wrote that he remembered me affectionately. So much for my faulty memories and classifications into good guys and bad guys.

When we returned from Indonesia in 1987, physically exhausted by short careers in veterinary practice and international development, I applied to be a university professor at a veterinary college. Resistance, as the Borg says in *Star Trek,* is futile. I was finally coming around to being at home with my natural skills and the realities of domestic life.

Even as a professor of health sciences, I continued my struggle to reconcile the irreconcilable languages of scholars and poets. If my 1970 poem on death, "Mortal's Prayer," was framed by the Lord's Prayer, "The Time of Our Lives," the poem which opens my 1995 collection from McClelland & Stewart, *The Impossible Uprooting,* is rooted in a celebration of the Now. "I am having the time of my life / digging up an old pine stump / with my daughter / in the bright fall sunshine," the poem begins. "Everything I need to know about life / and death is in this moment."

The poem ends "as the roots lift free, I am dug in, / rooted, / earthworms, beetles, fungi, / bacilli all around me, / skittling up the spade handle toward me, singing: // Welcome home. / Your turn is next." Based on poems like this, one of my scientific colleagues called me a "Now-ist."

Behind the public writing and performing, my underlying angst about the pointlessness of writing, the darkness that surrounds us, the challenges of finding the right language to articulate that which remains unspoken, have continued to plague me. In 1999, apparently trying to reassure me, American poet Julia Kasdorf sent me a quote from Robert Frost: "The right word, it's just a matter of life and death; that's all!" I think she was trying to be helpful. Or empathic.

In 1997, before an international audience of epidemiologists in Paris, and as part of a presentation on complexity and health, I read a poem I'd written about Mad Cow Disease in which I explored how, even with the best science we have, tragic outcomes can spring from noble intentions.

The poem resonated with the audience and was later published in a journal called *Preventive Veterinary Medicine.*

While in Indonesia, in the mid 1980s, I had written continually. I had thought veterinary medicine and family dynamics would ground me, and they did. But in a different culture, caught in the confused, morally conflicted landscapes of what's been called international development, I continued to struggle with what was important to write about. For me, this reflected a need to go beyond the *Good Housekeeping* and Tante Tina family saga to find narratives that could accommodate the whole messy world in which we lived, to address the larger questions that Mary Bender had sent me into the world to solve. I wrote a draft novella, but given the responsibilities of my job and family, poetry and essays still dominated my public voice. But the scope expanded. Again, annoyingly, Tante Tina was helpful.

I used Tante Tina not just to tell stories about my Ukrainian-Mennonite history, but to connect that history to current events. In 1993, at the twentieth anniversary of the Writers' Union of Canada, I was asked to read "Tante Tina's Request to put Salman Rushdie on the Missionary Prayer List." Graeme Gibson suggested I do it in costume. At the time, I had never done this. So I went room to room in the dormitory at the university asking if someone had a dress I could borrow. Then, between the main course and the dessert, I went to the men's bathroom to change. Apart from the sagging breasts made of hand towels, I was told it was very convincing. I was simply introduced as a woman from southern Manitoba. The light was poor, and I offered my request for prayer in my best flat German accent, which I cannot speak, but had learned to mimic.

Later, I couldn't recall whose dress I had borrowed, and the next morning I had to stand up at the AGM and announce that I had a woman's dress from the previous night, but I couldn't remember her name. The response was predictable.

Nevertheless, however popular she might be, Tina was still a trap I couldn't seem to escape. She was a stage voice. She was absurd, a dress to hide behind. She was not me, and I wondered how long I would hide behind my mother's skirts. Would I ever be able to write in my own voice?

In 2019 (when Mary Bender was 92), after sending her the occasional

Christmas card, I worked up the courage to telephone her, my old professor. Not knowing how alert and thoughtful she might be as a nonagenarian, imagining, perhaps, an old lady dozing by the radio, I asked her if she was reading much. She said that she read *The New York Times* every day. And then she added that just the previous week she finally understood T.S. Eliot's *Four Quartets*. This tugged at memories of my first published poem. I don't recall ever formally being taught T.S. Eliot. What little I knew of him had to do with wastelands, the cruel month of April, cats, magi, and hollow men. I tried reading his work again, and found my attention coming and going, like Eliot's women, talking of Michelangelo.

She recounted how, after being late in purchasing a ticket for Eliot's lecture at Orchestra Hall in Chicago, she thought she would be up in the back of the third balcony but was "forced" to sit on the stage. That was the only place that was available. So she was right beside T.S. Eliot, and, at 92, still recalled vividly when he said, "'And then, light.' And he just beamed. And he started reading *Four Quartets*."

After this conversation, I decided that I needed to go home and seriously read Four Quartets. I struggled to find insight in those wordy poems. Maybe I wasn't old enough? But then, in the dense shrubbery, I began to see images bright as Bohemian Waxwings, flitting twig to twig, or, as Eliot wrote, "the hidden laughter of children in the foliage."

My encounter with Mary Eleanor, like her own 1950s experience of Eliot, was a sort of epiphany, a stunning sense of light, and release, and peace. Another baptism. As one who grew up in an evangelical community, I recognized this as the tear-filled, heart-wrenching salvation experience of an altar call. It is also the peace that can come with Yoga, or transcendental or Vipassana meditation. And precisely because these being-in-the-moment experiences are untethered from specific religious doctrines, as well as from past or future, they are available to anyone. To understand *Four Quartets*, then, is to understand there is a lifetime burning in every moment, that all time, past and future, is here, now, and that language cannot hold this in any coherent fashion.

If musician John Cage and his fellows, dismayed at the constraints of language and the artifices of art, asked us all to traipse out into the woods and gather mushrooms, then T.S. Eliot struggled to use the straining, near-breaking words of poetry to embrace that core contradiction at the still point of life. In an anecdote which may be apocryphal, but which nonetheless rings true, Eliot was once asked by one of his readers what the poem meant, to which he replied, "If I could have articulated it more clearly, I would have done so." I have heard musicians wrestle with the same conundrum when someone asks, well this piece by Bach is wonderful, but what does it mean?

For many years, in teaching courses on public health, I argued that if one understood something, one should be able to explain it. As I struggled with my reading of *Four Quartets*, I was no longer so sure. What happens when you reach the limits of language? Some artists and writers, like Eliot, shift (some might say retreat) to symbolism and ritual—hence his self-described Anglo-Catholic orientation—which have their own unwieldy burdens.

I wondered if the mental connection I had made from T.S. Eliot to John Cage was too far-fetched, an academic conceit. But two years later, in an August 18, 2021 phone conversation with Mary Eleanor, she explained that she'd finally understood *Four Quartets* when she let go of the literal meaning of the words and felt the rhythm of the poetry. The meaning was in the rhythm. This understanding, it seemed to me, arose as much from some spiritual and academic crises as it did from the text itself.

"It's like raindrops falling through the sky," she said. "You just experience one drop after the other. And you don't try to make them make literal sense. Eliot's poetry is a dance. We don't know much about a still point. We always want to have words to make them logical. We tend to mistrust intuitive meanings. And mystery, and everything at that level, is hard for Mennonites." I suggested that this was not just true for Mennonites, but is a characteristic of the modern world, built around the language of computers, which is all based on ones and zeros. "Yes," she agreed. "Everything is [seen as] binary. Which is it, this or that? And we've got to know, exactly which it is, and follow that and not be caught dead with the other."

In *Burnt Norton*, the first of the quartets, Eliot offers this:

> At the still point of the turning world. Neither flesh nor fleshless;
> Neither from nor towards; at the still point, there the dance is,
>
> . . .

Neither ascent nor decline. Except for the point, the still point,
There would be no dance, and there is only the dance.

In returning to Eliot, and to my conversations with Mary Eleanor, I have been reminded of Rabindranath Tagore's *Gitanjali,* in which he wrote: "From the words of the poet men take what meanings please them; yet their last meaning points to thee." In not giving "Thee" a name, Tagore's embrace of that illuminating point is similar to the ambiguity of the "I Am Being" in Moses' burning bush, or the lover in Songs of Solomon.

Here's the rub, then: such experiences can make you a better soldier, killer, mountain climber, runner, lover, parent, veterinarian, butcher.

I raised these troubling thoughts to Mary Eleanor in our 2021 phone conversation—Eliot's antisemitism, for instance, and patriarchal attitudes. Many influential people, from Saint Paul and Gandhi, to Degas, Dickens, Wagner, Picasso, and Heidegger expressed despicable attitudes yet produced important works of art, theology, action, and philosophy. What do we do with that? Separate the work from the person?

"No," Mary Eleanor insisted, "We're all mixed up. That's what it means to be human." And then, as if her mind were grappling with the many facets of this ancient dilemma, and pondering perhaps someone she knew or the turbulent 60s and 70s during which we encountered each other, that time when The Revolution was coming that would change everything, she added that "in social action it is dangerous to think we have the right answer." I asked if the protests against the right-wing populist George Wallace, that occurred nearby while she was a professor, changed anything. She said, "Oh the protests during those days changed everything!"

"For the better?" I asked.

"That's ambiguous," she said emphatically. "It's hard," she finally added. "Often the best things are done in the hardest way."

More than half a century ago, Pablo Neruda looked out his window in Berlin at a "dirty, disgruntled winter" day, when ten horses stepped into his line of vision. Like a good poet (and a good scientist), he saw the horses and observed them carefully. But he saw more. He saw that "the horses' intense presence was blood, / was rhythm, was the beckoning Grail of being . . . the fire that sprang to life in beautiful things."

"You do not have to be good," says Mary Oliver in "Wild Geese," which is a huge relief and comfort to me. But we have an obligation to be real, and maybe, to be better. To care about what Neruda, in "Horses," called "the fire that sprang to life in beautiful things," as well as the beauty that springs to life in the misshapen, the fallen, the ugly.

When I am consulted as an expert on pandemics or zoonoses, and when I care for, and talk to, my small flock of backyard chickens, I think about *Four Quartets*.

Poetry, for me, has become a way to converse with my experience of raw, complex reality in the midst of all the narratives, scientific, and logical explanations I use to try to understand it. It is a way of making noise to keep the bears away, of speaking to the deep spirit of cow dung, pandemics, cocky chickens, and rave-dancing primary-numbered cicadas, of arguing with the gods, singing in the dark, trying to out-shout the yapping yowling all-night dogs outside my hotel window in Nairobi until I awake, exhausted, nervous, and full of hope. It is, finally, an immersion into the murkiness of daily life, and a rising up to radiant possibilities.

NOTES

These reflections have been pillaged and rewritten and repackaged from previous publications including (among others): *The New Quarterly* (several volumes); *Poetry and Spiritual Practice* (Susan McCaslin, ed.); *Poetry as Liturgy* (Margot Swiss, ed.), *Journal of the Center for Mennonite Writing* ("The Professor, Four Quartets, and an Epiphany").

Nick Lindsay was included in Studs Terkel's collection of interviews with American workers, *Working: People Talk About What They Do All Day and How They Feel About What They Do* (Pantheon Books, 1974).

Works that set the foundations: The complete poetry of W.B. Yeats, William Blake, Dylan Thomas, and John Donne. Pier Giorgio di Cicco's *The Tough Romance* and *Flying Deeper into the Century*. The European romantics: Keats, Percy Shelley, Wordsworth, Byron. Goethe, especially his galloping "Erlkönig". Rabindranath Tagore's *Gitanjali*.

Works that carried me forward: All of Pablo Neruda. All of Mary Oliver. Whitman's *Leaves of Grass*; Gary Snyder's *The Back Country*;

Lawrence Ferlinghetti's *Starting from San Francisco*; all of Leonard Cohen; all of Bob Dylan; Anne Sexton's *Transformations*; Seamus Heaney's *Death of a Naturalist*; James Fenton's *The Memory of War* and *Children in Exile*; Jeni Couzyn's *Christmas in Africa*; Al Purdy's *Selected*.

WORKS CITED

Dostoyevsky, Fyodor. *The Brothers Karamazov*. 1880. Translated by Constance Garnett, Heinemann, 1912.

Eliot, T.S. *Four Quartets*. 1943. Faber & Faber, 2019.

Frankfurt, Harry G. *On Bullshit*, Princeton University Press, 2005.

Neruda, Pablo. "Horses." Translated by Alastair Reid. *A New Decade: Poems 1958-1967*, Grove Press, 1968.

Oliver, Mary. "Wild Geese." *Dream Work*, Atlantic Monthly Press, 1994.

p'Bitek, Okot. *The Song of Lawino*, Modern African Library, 1968.

Shelley, Percy Bysshe. "Ozymandias." *The Complete Poetical Works of Percy Bysshe Shelley*, Oxford University Press, 1919.

Tagore, Rabindranath. *Gitanjali (Song Offerings)*, translated by Tagore, India Society, 1912.

Waltner-Toews, David. "Animal Farm Comes to America." *Thirteen Poets*, edited by Harley King, Pinchpenny Press, 1971.

---. "Uncaged." ["Circus Animal."] *That Inescapable Animal*, Pinchpenny Press, 1974.

---. "The Time of our Lives." *The Impossible Uprooting*, McClelland & Stewart, 1995.

ACKNOWLEDGEMENTS AND NOTES

I would especially like to thank The Writers Union of Canada. For decades, they have provided guidance on negotiating contracts, worked energetically to improve Canada's copyright laws, and through their programs for Writers in the Schools and National Public Readings provided opportunities and support to perform my work and interact with other writers in venues across Canada. And I'd like to thank Sue Sorensen of CMU Press for inviting me to be part of this illustrious Lyrik series.

***The Earth is One Body* (Turnstone Press, 1979)**
Confessions of a Tourist Without a Camera
Homestead
The True Meaning of Being a Man

Original note:

- Special thanks to the Saskatoon Poets Group, and to the editors at Turnstone, who helped me with much of the fine tuning in this work.

***Good Housekeeping* (Turnstone Press, 1983)**
The Door
Emmanuel
The Next Ten Years
The Poetry of Work
Sweeping

***Endangered Species* (Turnstone Press, 1988)**
We are grateful for the permission granted by Turnstone Press to include in the present book poems originally published in *Endangered Species*.

Conversion Experience
Endangered Species
Generations
Identifying a Tree in the Fall
The Mind
November Light

Peaceful Linguistics
A Poem for Giorgio
Something is Missing
Still Life, with a Mango
What to Pray For

Original note:

- Some of these poems previously appeared in *Mennonite Blues*, a stage adaptation of the poems of David Waltner-Toews by Larry Danielson.

***The Impossible Uprooting* (McClelland & Stewart, 1995)**
Bird of Prey
Breaking Free the Whales
The Ecology of Poetry
The Gift
Natural Love
The Snow Fort
The Time of Our Lives

Original notes:

- Special thanks to Stan Dragland for his editorial guidance, and to Ellen Seligman at M&S for midwifing this book into the world.
- On "Breaking Free the Whales": In 1988, an international mission was organized to rescue several whales separated from their pod and trapped in the arctic ice off Alaska. The action was massive, expensive, and probably, ultimately, detrimental to the wild population of whales, and made a great many people feel good about themselves. It was typical, in other words, not only of how we usually show our affection for nature, but for each other.

***The Fat Lady Struck Dumb* (Brick Books, 2000)**
Beached
A Bill from the Power Company
Death of a Humanist
Death of a Naturalist
The Fat Lady Struck Dumb
How the Earth Loves You

A Man Sits Naked
My Mother's Heart Attack
On the Death of a Father
A Post-Cambrian Lament
Sunday Morning
Teilhard de Chardin Surfs the Internet
You are Not a Cat

Original notes:

- Many of these poems were written for particular people, and read at specific occasions (birthdays, graduations, anniversaries, weddings, workshops on complexity, conferences, etc.). The people who received those poems know who they are, and, with a few exceptions, I have chosen not to distract the reader with their names. Not sure if a particular poem was written for you? If the poem fits, wear it.
- Special thanks to Stan Dragland, for helping to keep me in tune.

***The Complete Tante Tina: Mennonite Blues and Recipes* (Pandora Press, 2004)**
Haenschen's Complaint
Haenschen's Success
How a Story Made Little Haenschen and Angela Get Married
Roots
Tante Tina Calls in to a Canadian Radio Talk Show
Tante Tina Out of Time
Tante Tina Reflects on Maggie Thatcher
Tante Tina Remembers Trudeau
Tante Tina Talks about Her Man
Tante Tina Tells a Bible Story
Tante Tina's Christmas
Tante Tina's Lament

Original note:

- Tante Tina first made her appearance in *Canadian Forum* in 1979. Many of these poems were included in *The Impossible Uprooting*. "Englische" is a generic term Tina and her family use for anyone who isn't a Mennonite.

The Gravity of Love **(St. Thomas Poetry Series, 2023)**
We are grateful for the permission granted by St. Thomas Poetry Series to include in the present book poems originally published in *The Gravity of Love*.

Chicken Soup
Faith for the Long Trek Out of Olduvai
For what we are about to receive
Milton Hikes the Bruce Trail
Trees

Original notes:

- "Chicken Soup" (as "Chicken Soup for the Body") appeared in other versions in my books *Food, Sex, and Salmonella* (Greystone, 2008) and *A Conspiracy of Chickens* (Wolsak and Wynn, 2022). "Trees" (as "For the Love of Trees"), "Faith for the Long Trek Out of Olduvai" (as "Fill Your Mind with Elephants"), "For what we are about to receive" and "Milton Hikes the Bruce Trail" (as "Conversations with Nature") were included in *Poetry as Liturgy*, edited by Margo Swiss (St. Thomas Poetry Series, 2007).
- A special thanks to David Kent for taking a chance on a poet who hasn't had a book of poetry out in more than 20 years, and to David Kent and Hildi Froese Tiessen for their fine-grained reading and deft editing.

Notes for uncollected and new poems

- "At Dusk, a Merchant" was commissioned for *Drawing Near* as part of the Anabaptism at 500 suite published by MennoMedia, 2025. Used by permission.
- "The Way of Memories" was published in *The American Journal of Nursing* in 1973.

INDEX OF POEMS